High School American Literature

A collection of readings and activities

for a full year American Literature curriculum.

Grades 10-12

THE AUTHOR'S MEMORIES.

Michelle Deerwester-Dalrymple

ISBN: 9798859308507
Imprint: Independently published

Formatting by Michelle Deerwester- Dalrymple

Images licensed by Canva

All of the readings included are readily and freely available through open-courseware and open online sources including Poetry.com, Poets.com, the Gutenberg Project, American Literature.com,and the Internet Archive.

American Literature/9-12th grade English:

This course is set as a college prep, academic literature course, yearlong study. Students will complete a significant amount of reading during the course - many times reading a larger novel while discussing short stories or poetry of the same literary period. These studies will include elements such as: character, conflict, theme, symbolism, and literary devices, for a comprehensive analysis of literature. *Please note this is a secular text, and different ideologies reflected in American Literature is reflected, but to understand Colonialism better, a brief overview of some of their religious tenants is included. This can be skipped if the parent/teacher does not feel it necessary to include it.*

Students will write 5 papers total, including one longer MLA formatted research paper over the course of the year. Novel readings will include the use of study guides, and the shorter readings will include in class and take home "journal" homework.

Vocabulary can often be invaluable with a more advanced study of literature and writing. If you wish to include a vocabulary component to help student develop their written voice, I recommend *Vocabulary through the Classical Roots*. You can also select a grammar program of your choice to add to this text if you desire your student to have a more thorough understanding of grammar structures.

To make the text more accessible and economical, the text uses the links to additional resources, specifically novel and author study guides. The links are listed below.

Novel Studies, complete with study guide activities:

- *A Scarlet Letter* by Hawthorne
- *The Adventures of Huckleberry Finn* - Twain
- *Grapes of Wrath* – Steinbeck OR *Raisin in the Sun* - Hansberry (parent/student choice)
- *Old man and the Sea* by Hemmingway

Poetry, Short Stories, and Speeches – in class activities, short writing/responses and homework related to literary devices and study of Movements in American Literature (here is a sample):

Native American myth, "Sinners in the hands of an Angry God" by Edwards, Poetry of Anne Bradstreet, Writings of Thomas Paine, " Legend of Sleepy Hollow" by Irving; "The Raven" by Edgar Allen Poe, Longfellow poetry, Holmes Poetry, "solitude" by Thoreau; Poetry of Emily Dickinson, "leaves of Grass" excerpt, "O Captain My Captain" by Walt Whitman; "I will fight no more forever" Speech, "Man with a hoe" by Markham; "The Last Leaf" by O Henry, TS Eliot –" Love Song of J Alfred Prufrock", "The Yellow Wallpaper" by Gilman; Langston Hughes poetry, "A jury of her peers" by Susan Gladspell , Poetry of Maya Angelou and Shel Silverstein

Students will keep a **literature** journal for most in class writing assignments and homework. Each journal entry needs a title (e.g "Native myths Journal 1," etc). Journals can be complete with the parent/instructor in class or can be assigned for the student to do on their own. Each Journal assignment is due the following week.

Novel Study guides will be turned in with a paper when we complete the novel. There will be four Novel Studies for the semester. Again, these can be completed by the student with or without the parent/instructor's assistance. They can be graded weekly or once the entire study guide is completed.

There will be a 5 major writing assignments – Literary response essays to the novels are 4 of the 5 major writing assignments.

NOTE: This text also includes the Research Essay outline workbook in Appendix 6.

DEVICES WORKSHEET:

At the end of this text is a rhetorical devices worksheet, which is titled **Devices worksheet** throughout this text. Your student will use it in tandem with other journal and writing assignments. First, they will review the different types of devices. You can do a section each week so all the devices are covered early in the year, or you can break it up and review 3-4 devices each week and focus on those.

When the assignment calls for the **Devices worksheet,** the student will review possible devices they see in the writing, review the devices worksheet to identify more, then note the devices in the Journal homework, and from the writing include an example on the Devices worksheet. The student will then use the Devices worksheet as a study and reference guide.

For "Discuss" activities listed in the schedule, the student can do the following: go over the instructional information in this text, review completed study guide material together, review completed journal activities, have the student do internet research on the time period or author and read/share it with the parent.

Appendices: Several appendices appear at the end of this text. They are references for story elements to be discussed or referenced in the text. The appendices include an overview of story elements, an overview of conflict, a grading rubric for essays, the quizzes and keys, and the answer sheet for the journal activities.

** For added information and detail about authors or movements in American Literature, please go to YouTube and access John Greene's Crash Course in American Literature playlist. It's fun and educational!**

Students should be prepared with the following:

1. A three ring binder
2. A notebook or composition book that will fit in the binder (3 hole punched) OR Dividing Tabs and loose notebook paper
3. 2-3 Folders that are three hole punched and can fit into the binder
4. Pens/pencils, a set of colored pens, and a set of highlighter pens (you can get all this cheap at the dollar store!)
5. Access to a computer or tablet or readings, research, and essay writing.

Links for longer stories and novels:

Semester 1:

Scarlet Letter -- http://www.planetpublish.com/wp-content/uploads/2011/11/The_Scarlet_Letter_T.pdf

> Study Guide:
> https://drive.google.com/file/d/1axykkT0OQ6kv6bbzsZ0H2JavVSElD3gQ/view?usp=sharing

Legend of Sleepy Hollow – http://www.ibiblio.org/ebooks/Irving/Sleepy/Irving_Sleepy.pdf

> Irving study guide:
> https://drive.google.com/file/d/1oFgGdy9SyN6XJvqPCU8PZkEW8W1GXbsJ/view?usp=sharing

Thoreau's Walden Ch 5 Solitude –
https://docs.google.com/document/d/1pYiO6yu7NgL0iiNzE8hQMCcJjxd9wJSff137ld9kNiM/edit?usp=sharing

The Adventures of Huckleberry Finn – http://contentserver.adobe.com/store/books/HuckFinn.pdf

Study Guide: https://drive.google.com/file/d/160WwH1jFJEosvKFB-TqD0AmRlvWHi78L/view?usp=sharing

Semester 2:

The Yellow Wallpaper: https://www.gutenberg.org/cache/epub/1952/pg1952-images.html

The Last Leaf -- https://americanenglish.state.gov/files/ae/resource_files/the-last-leaf.pdf

Grapes of Wrath (book option 1) -- https://archive.org/details/in.ernet.dli.2015.261773/page/n9/mode/2up

Interactive Study Guide: https://docs.google.com/document/d/1ZaH4cRpDqcrh0zlosdG-cfgWo3xfuWrP/edit?usp=sharing&ouid=111553973189563884096&rtpof=true&sd=true

Raisin in the Sun (book option 2) --https://drive.google.com/file/d/1NKT6-JsTAhuIjxGMMiZilskL6yAg9Sqx/view?usp=sharing

Interactive Study Guide: https://docs.google.com/document/d/1VP49F-VHNGpLSohm43TAXwgZrL-71UUl/edit?usp=sharing&ouid=111553973189563884096&rtpof=true&sd=true

Jury of her Peers -- https://americanliterature.com/author/susan-glaspell/short-story/a-jury-of-her-peers

Harrison Bergeron -- http://wordfight.org/bnw/bnw-unit_packet.pdf

Old Man and the Sea –https://gutenberg.ca/ebooks/hemingwaye-oldmanandthesea/hemingwaye-oldmanandthesea-00-h.html

Study Guide: https://drive.google.com/file/d/12l8998Y5ZVR50r6johwHudr9OaLD1Nrl/view?usp=sharing

Many of these links are on a Google Drive website for easy access as well. You can also elect to purchase all of the novels and short stories separately – through Amazon or your favorite retailer – or borrowed through the library. If you cannot access a document or a link as gone done, please don't hesitate to reach out to the author at mddalrympleauthor@gmail.com

Grading:		total points
Writing Journal assignments -	10 pts each	240 pts
A final quiz	40 pts	40 pts
Writing Assignments (4 total)	100 pts each	400 pts
Study Guides (4) total	20 pts each	80 pts
Major Research Paper	200 pts	200 pts
Total points for the class		960 points

Table of Contents

Unit One: Pre Colonial and Colonial Literature: 7 weeks

Week 1:
- Discuss Devices worksheet and literature
- Introduction of Novel Study (4 weeks reading plus paper for week 5-7) – Scarlet Letter. Use the study guide link on page XX
- Begin of overview of Native American Myths in text pp XX
  - Homework: Complete **Journal (1) Paradoxes**
    - Read all three myths in text .
    - Read **Chapters 1-5 in Scarlet Letter (book).** Work corresponding **study guide** pages

Week 2:
- Discuss introductory elements of Scarlet Letter. Discuss conflict – **see Appendix 1 on Conflict**
- Discuss the **Native American Myths** and complete activity in journal (2)
- Review the first five chapters of **Scarlet Letter** with the student.
  - Homework:
    - Read Chapters 6-11 in Scarlet Letter. Work on corresponding Study Guide pages

Week 3:
- Discuss themes in Literature and **Colonialism** and Colonial religion on pg XX
- Scarlet Letter – discuss characters, motives, sin, Poetic devices worksheet, and study guide through Ch 11
  - Homework:
    - Read "Sinners in the Hands of an Angry God" In packet - summarize main ideas.
    - Read Chapters 12-16 in Scarlet Letter. Work on Study guide.

Week 4:
- Discuss elements of **Colonial Literature** and "Sinners . . .". **Journal activity (3).**
- Scarlet Letter – Discuss themes/Devices, characters, reflections on society, and conflict through Ch 16.
- Go over essay ideas sheet for the first class essay (thesis resources are in Appendix 5)
  - Homework: Read "To my Dear and Loving Husband" by Anne Bradstreet in packet
    - Read Chapters 17-21 in Scarlet Letter – work on study guide. Have student work on "Thesis" worksheet in appendix)
    - Begin thinking of paper choice – it is due Week 8

Week 5:
- Discuss paper for Scarlet letter- how to establish a thesis
- Bradstreet Poetry in class – Devices worksheet **– Journal Activity (4).**
  - Homework: Read the Thomas Paine excerpt in packet
    - Read Chapters 22-24 (end) in Scarlet Letter
    - Work on paper ideas – write a thesis for your paper and write down 3 quotes from book that support or show what you claim. Write down why you think these quotes show this. Use Devices worksheet to help identify devices that support your ideas.

Week 6:
- Scarlet letter- develop introduction and body paragraphs/theme and conflict
- Discuss **Age of Enlightenment** and Thomas Paine in class.
  - Homework: Work on Scarlet Letter **Paper** – Due in two weeks week!

- Scarlet Letter **study guide** due in two weeks
- Read "The Crisis" In packet

Week 7:
- Finish working on Sermon
- Finish discussing Thomas Paine in class **–Journal (5)**
- Discuss "Leads" activity
  - Homework:
    - Read " "Legend of Sleepy Hollow" online book pages 1-20 – use link.
    - Complete **Revolution/Kipling activity Journal (6)**
    - Scarlet letter paper and study guide due next week!

Unit Two Romantic Literature: 7 weeks

Week 8:
- **Scarlet Letter Paper and study guide Due!**
- Discuss Romanticism – Discuss Romantic elements from *The Scarlet Letter*
- Legend of Sleepy Hollow first part review/conflict/theme – **begin Journal Activity (7)**.
  - Homework:
    - Finish "Legend . . ." pages 21-41
    - Complete Sleepy Hollow questions in **Journal (7)**

Week 9:
- Discuss **Romantic** elements in *Sleepy Hollow* – use Devices worksheet
- Introduce Poe and *the Raven*/Gothic Romantic
  - Homework:
    - Read "The Raven" by Poe in packet. Identify devices and add to devices worksheet as necessary to help with next week's journal.

Week 10:
- Discuss **Romantic** elements from *Raven* -Devices worksheet
- "The Raven" review/conflict/imagery/theme – **Journal Activity - Poe (8)**.
  - Homework:
    - **Finish Journal (8) Poe**
    - Read "Hiawatha" by Longfellow in packet – Identify devices for class
    -

Week 11:
- Discuss **Fireside** elements from Hiawatha - add to devices worksheet
- "Old Ironsides" introduction
  - Homework:
    - Read "Old Ironsides" by Holmes in packet – Identify devices
    - "Hiawatha" and "Old Ironsides" – **Journal Activity (9)**.

Week 12:
- Discuss **Fireside** elements from Old Ironside
- Discuss **Transcendentalism**
- **Paradox activity -- Journal Activity (10)**.
  - Homework: Read Emily Dickenson from Packet
    - Discuss Journal #9..

Week 13:
- Discuss **Writing Assignment #2** (with creative art option) – students can read ahead for an author not yet discussed.
- **Lyrical Poetry** and Emily Dickinson/imagery/theme

- Complete Dickenson activity in class– **Journal Activity (11)**.
  - Read Walden Ch 5 "Solitude" by Thoreau – use link

Week 14:
- Discuss *Solitude* – identify paradoxes as you have learned them this semester. **Journal (12)**
- Rhetorical devices overview. Identify devices used in literature thus far
  - Homework:
    - Begin Reading Huck Finn chapters 1-5 (it's a lot – the book is long. Pace yourself and work on **the study guide** AS YOU READ)
    - Select your author for Writing assignment #2 -- **due week 16!**
    - Read Walt Whitman Oh Captain My Captain/ Song of Myself in packet

Unit 3 – Realism and the Turn of the Century (6 weeks) END OF SEMESTER ONE
Week 15:
- Discuss Walt Whitman
- **Realism** overview and Huck Finn intro activity/conflict –
  - Homework: **Journal Activity (13)**
    - Continue working on writing assignment #2
    - Huck Finn – chapters 6-15 (work on **study guide**!)

Week 16:
- **Writing/Art Project for Romantic period due by the end of the week!**
- **Journal Activity (14) Uncle Tom's cabin**
- Discuss Twain and how he presented realism
  - Homework:
    - Huck Finn – chapters 15-22 (work on **study guide**!)

Week 17:
- Devices worksheet in class for Dickenson and Twain – You can print a clean version of the Devices Worksheet if needed.
- **Romantic and Free verse** – Walt Whitman/imagery/theme – **start Journal Activity (15)**.
- Discuss Huck Finn and study guide thus far. Review Realism and Huck Finn essay #3
  - Homework:
    - Huck Finn – chapters 23-31 (work on study guide)
    - Read Whitman's Leaves of Grass excerpts in packet
    - **Journal Activity – Gettysburg address (14)**.

Week 18:
- Walt Whitman/imagery/theme **Finish Journal (15)**
- Devices worksheet in class
- Begin Realism essay #3
  - Homework:
    - Huck Finn – chapters 32-end (finish text and study guide)
    - Read Chief Joseph "I will fight no more forever" in packet
    - Work on Realism Essay #3

Week 19:

- Discuss Chief Joseph/worksheet. How does this show realism? – Realism diary entries -**Journal Activity (16)**.
- Discuss elements/themes etc. for Huck Finn. Review Essay Question options/write thesis statement.
  - ○ Homework:
    - ▪ Work on Essay #3 at home.
    - ▪ Complete **study guide** if you have not already. It will be due with your paper.
    - ▪ Read Markham's "Man with a Hoe" in packet

Week 20:
- Work on Huck Finn paper in class. Review body paragraphs, and conclusions.
- Discuss **naturalism**, worker's issues, industrialism, and how the poetry reflects that.
- Devices worksheet in class-- **Realism** activity – **journal (17)**
  - ○ Homework:
    - ▪ Finish paper – it is **due next week.**
    - ▪ **Study guide** due next week.

Unit 4 – Early 20th Century and the rise of the Moderns
Week 21:
- **Huck Finn Paper #3 and Study guide due!**
- Begin Discussion of the **Modern era** in writing.
- **Review and start Research Paper in Appendix 5 – begin research!**
  - ○ Homework:
    - ▪ Begin Reading "The last leaf" – use the link.
    - ▪ Begin Reading Grapes of Wrath Chapters 1-8/Raisin Act 1– **Interactive Study guide**

Week 22:
- Discuss issues and themes for turn of the century
- **Prufrock** activity – **journal (18)**
- **Review and start Research Paper in Appendix 5 – begin research!**
- Discuss "The last leaf" – theme/reflection of era/ devices –**Journal Activity (18)**.
  - ○ Homework
    - ▪ Read "Yellow Wallpaper" by Gilman—use the link
    - ▪ Grapes chapters 9-16/Raisin Act 2 – **Interactive study guide**

Week 22:
- Discuss "Yellow Wallpaper." Compare to Last Leaf – which has a hopeful ending?
- Devices worksheet with current readings
  - ○ Homework:
    - ▪ Read "Love Song of J Alfred Prufrock" by TS Eliot
    - ▪ Read Grapes chapter 17-23/Raisin Act 3 – **Interactive study guide**
    - ▪ **Work on Research essay – complete research and notes section**

Week 23:
- Discuss Love Song and elements of modernist poetry
- Review allusions and connect to Eliot's philosophy– **Prufrock Journal Activity (19)**.
- Review Research essay thesis /idea. Have student start writing notes
  - ○ Homework:
    - ▪ Read William Carlos Williams and Robert Frost
    - ▪ Finish Grapes chapter 24-30/Finish Raisin – **Interactive study guide**
    - ▪ Continue working Research paper –**complete notes**

        ■

Week 24:
- Discuss Williams Carlos Williams and imagist poetry/ Frost and **naturalism**. – **Modern Poetry Journal # 20**
- Work on Devices worksheet. Compare the above to Prufrock and **modernism**.
- Work on paper in class- review their notes and have student begin outline and paragraphs
  - ○ Homework: Read Langston Hughes – identify Harlem Renaissance elements.
    - ■ Work on paper at home. **Due in Three weeks** – you get one extra week to work on this paper since it is longer and requires research! Work on **completing outline and paragraphs**

Week 25:
- Discuss **The Harlem Renaissance** and its themes.
- Devices worksheet -- Discuss Langston Hughes –Take a biblical verse or parable and convey it in a jazz/Harlem renaissance sense - **Journal Activity (21)**.
- Work on paper elements.
  - ○ Homework:
    - ■ Work on Research paper! Due in two weeks-- Work on finalizing paragraphs into a full draft and on citation..

Week 26:
- Paper workshop in class. Review that students are meeting the requirements for the paper. – Review rough draft of essay.
- Review Journal 21
  - ○ Homework: **Finish Research Paper!**
    - ■ **Study Guide for Grapes/ Raisin Due!**

Unit 5 - Post War/Post Modern :
Week 27:
- **RESEARCH PAPER DUE!**
- Discuss **Post Modern Era** -
  - ○ Homework:
    - ■ Begin <u>Old man and the Sea</u> by Hemmingway – Beginning through "dreams" and Study Guide
    - ■ Read "a Jury of her Peers" by Susan Gladspell Link. **(Journal 22)**

Week 28:
- Discuss **Post Modern Era** and Discuss Jury of her Peers – add to literary devices
  - ○ Homework:
    - ■ Continue <u>Old man and the Sea</u> "Presentation of the sea" through "the man and Nature" by Hemmingway and Study Guide
    - ■ Read "Harrison Bergeron" by Kurt Vonnegut Jr (link)

Week 29:
- Discuss how Harrison Bergeron is **Post Modernist**
- Discuss Old Man and Sea – in class activity.
- Begin Response essay #4
  - ○ Homework:
    - ■ Finish <u>Old man and the Sea</u> "Santiago" through end of book and Study Guide
    - ■ Review writing activities for Modern/ Post Modern Era. Select a topic to write a short 1-2 page response.

- Read Maya Angelou

Week 30:
- Discuss Hemingway / Discuss Maya Angelou **(Journal 23)**
- Discuss response paper.
  - ○ Homework:
    - Work on Final response paper – it is due in two weeks/last day of class.
    - Read Shel Silverstein in packet

Week 31:
- Discuss Shel Silverstein and favorite current writers
- **Final Journal #24** -- Imagination
- **Study guide**
  - ○ Homework: Study for final exam in class.
    - Complete on Final response paper

Week 32:
- **Turn in final Response Paper!**
- Take Final Literature quiz!!! Have a great summer!

•

Lesson Planner

(make copies as necessary)

Week:	Readings	Activities	Assessment
Monday			
Tuesday			
Wednesday			
Thursday			
Friday			

American Literature Overview

There are many different literary movements and not everyone agrees on what qualifies things to be a movement. There are also arguments as to where certain pieces of literature fit into the grand scheme of things. We will look at several movements here along with information about some of the smaller movements:

1. **Puritan/Colonial (1650-1750)**

2. **Revolutionary/Age of Reason (1750-1800)**

3. **Romanticism (1800-1860)**

4. **American Renaissance/ Transcendentalism (1840-1860)**

5. **Realism (1855-1900)**

6. **The Moderns (1900-1950)**

7. **Harlem Renaissance (1920s)**

8. **Post-Modernism (1950 to present)**

9. **Contemporary (1970s-Present)**

Paradox Information and Pre-activity

Literature often uses paradoxes to make a point, show a double standard, or highlight an irony in life or the world. This year, we will look at several examples of paradox and at how paradoxes are used in American Literature. You can use one of these examples to fill out the Paradox segment of your Devices worksheet.

A definition of paradox:

a seemingly absurd or self-contradictory statement or proposition that when investigated or explained may prove to be well founded or true.

Journal #1: Introduction to Paradoxes:

Below are two scenarios that each feature a paradox. Write a short explanation of why each is a paradox.

1. Scientists have discovered time travel. John goes back in time to 1900 and meets his great-grandfather as a young child. John invites the boy to see the circus. Unfortunately, there's an accident at the circus which paralyzes the boy from his neck down. What is the paradox?

2. Leslie tells her friends at school that she lost her cell phone at the basketball game that afternoon. "If you find it, call or text me." What is the paradox?

Unit 1: Pre Colonial and Colonial Literature
Native Myths

Native tribes in America date back for tens of thousands of years. Much of their belief systems are based on a natural understanding of the world. Their myths and stories reflect those natural elements. This movement is based mostly on oral tradition – which can give us a hint as to why there is very little written material
Those stories, fables, tales, myths and chants were written down later for preservation, not because that was typical for Native Americans of the time. Nature and elements of nature are the most common aspect of Native American writings

When Grizzlies Walked Upright - Modoc

Before there were people on earth, the Chief of the Sky Spirits grew tired of his home in the Above World, because the air was always brittle with an icy cold. So he carved a hole in the sky with a stone and pushed all the snow and ice down below until he made a great mound that reached from the earth almost to the sky. Today it is known as Mount Shasta.

Then the Sky Spirit took his walking stick, stepped from a cloud to the peak, and walked down to the mountain. When he was about halfway to the valley below, he began to put his finger to the ground here and there, here and there. Wherever his finger touched, a tree grew. The snow melted in his footsteps, and the water ran down in rivers.

The Sky Spirit broke off the small end of his giant stick and threw the pieces into the rivers. The longer pieces turned into beaver and otter; the smaller pieces became fish. When the leaves dropped from the trees, he picked them up, blew upon them, and so made the birds. Then he took the big end of his giant stick and made all the animals that walked on the earth, the biggest of which were the grizzly bears.

Now when they were first made, the bears were covered with hair and had sharp claws, just as they do today, but they walked on two feet and could talk like people. They looked so fierce that the Sky Spirit sent them away from him to live in the forest at the base of the mountain.

Pleased with what he'd done, the Chief of the Sky Spirits decided to bring his family down and live on earth himself. The mountains of snow and ice became their lodge. He made a big fire in the center of the mountain and a hole in the top so that the smoke and sparks could fly out. When he put a big log on the fire, sparks would fly up and the earth would tremble.

Late one spring while the Sky Spirit and his family were sitting round the fire, the Wind Spirit sent a great storm that shook the top of the mountain. It blew and blew and roared and roared. Smoke blown back into the lodge hurt their eyes, and finally the Sky Spirit said to his youngest daughter, "Climb up to the smoke hole and ask the Wind Spirit to blow more gently. Tell him I'm afraid he will blow the mountain over."

As his daughter started up, her father said, "But be careful not to stick your head out at the top. If you do, the wind may catch you by the hair and blow you away."

The girl hurried to the top of the mountain and stayed well inside the smoke hole as she spoke to the Wind Spirit. As she was about to climb back down, she remembered that her father had once said you could see the ocean from the top of their lodge. His daughter wondered what the ocean looked like, and her curiosity got the better of her. She poked her head out of the hole and turned toward the west, but before she could see anything, the Wind Spirit caught her long hair, pulled her out of the mountain, and blew her down over the snow and ice. She landed among the scrubby fir trees at the edge of the timber and snow line, her long red hair trailing over the snow.

There a grizzly bear found the little girl when he was out hunting food for his family. He carried her home with him, and his wife brought her up with their family of cubs. The little red-haired girl and the cubs ate together, played together, and grew up together.

When she became a young woman, she and the eldest son of the grizzly bears were married. In the years that followed they had many children, who were not as hairy as the grizzlies, yet did not look exactly like their spirit mother, either.

All the grizzly bears throughout the forests were so proud of these new creatures that they made a lodge for the red-haired mother and her children. They placed the lodge near Mount Shasta-it is called Little Mount Shasta today.

After many years had passed, the mother grizzly bear knew that she would soon die. Fearing that she should ask of the Chief of the Sky Spirits to forgive her for keeping his daughter, she gathered all the grizzlies at the lodge they had built. Then she sent her eldest grandson in a cloud to the top of Mount Shasta, to tell the Spirit Chief where he could find his long-lost daughter.

When the father got this news he was so glad that he came down the Mountainside in giant strides, melting the snow and tearing up the land under his feet. Even today his tracks can be seen in the rocky path on the south side of Mount Shasta.

As he neared the lodge, he called out, "Is this where my little daughter lives?"

He expected his child to look exactly as she had when he saw her last. When he found a grown woman instead, and learned that the strange creatures she was taking care of were his grandchildren, he became very angry. A new race had been created that was not of his making! He frowned on the old grandmother so sternly that she promptly fell dead. Then he cursed all the grizzlies:

"Get down on your hands and knees. You have wronged me, and from this moment all of you will walk on four feet and never talk again."

He drove his grandchildren out of the lodge, put his daughter over his shoulder, and climbed back up the mountain. Never again did he come to the forest. Some say that he put out the fire in the center of his lodge and took his daughter back up to the sky to live.

Those strange creatures, his grandchildren, scattered and wandered over the earth. They were the first Indians, the ancestors of all the Indian tribes.

That's why the Indians living around Mount Shasta would never kill a grizzly bear. Whenever a grizzly killed an Indian, his body was burned on the spot. And for many years all who passed that way cast a stone there until a great pile of stones marked the place of his death.

The Earth on Turtle's Back

Onondaga   Retold by Michael Caduto and Joseph Bruchac

Before this Earth existed, there was only water. It stretched as far as one could see, and in that water there were birds and animals swimming around. Far above, in the clouds, there was a Skyland. In that Skyland there was a great and beautiful tree. It had four white roots which stretched to each of the sacred directions, and from its branches all kinds of fruits and flowers grew.

There was an ancient chief in the Skyland. His young wife was expecting a child, and one night she dreamed that she saw the Great Tree uprooted. The next day she told her husband the story.

He nodded as she finished telling her dream. "My wife," he said, "I am sad that you had this dream. It is clearly a dream of great power and, as is our way, when one has such a powerful dream we must do all we can to make it true. The Great Tree must be uprooted."

Then the ancient chief called the young men together and told them that they must pull up the tree. But the roots of the tree were so deep, so strong, that they could not budge it. At last the Ancient Chief himself came to the tree. He wrapped his arms around it, bent his knees and strained. At last, with one great effort, he uprooted the tree and placed it on its side. Where the tree's roots had gone deep into the Skyland there was now a big hole. The wife of the chief came close and leaned over to look down, grasping the tip of one of the Great Tree's branches to steady her. It seemed as if she saw something down there, far below, glittering like water. She leaned out further to look and, as she leaned, she lost her balance and fell into the hole. Her grasp slipped off the tip of the branch, leaving her with only a handful of seeds as she fell, down, down, down, down.

Far below, in the waters, some of the birds and animals looked up. "Someone is falling toward us from the sky," said one of the birds.

"We must do something to help her," said another. Then two Swans flew up. They caught the Woman From The Sky between their wide wings. Slowly, they began to bring her down toward the water, where the birds and animals were watching.

"She is not like us," said one of the animals. "Look, she doesn't have webbed feet. I don't think she can live in the water." "What shall we do then?" said another of the water animals.

"I know," said one of the water birds. "I have heard that there is Earth far below the waters. If we dive down and bring up Earth, then she will have a place to stand." So the birds and animal decided that someone would have to bring up Earth. One by one they tried. The Duck dove first, some say. He swam down and down, far beneath the surface, but could not reach the bottom and floated back up. Then the Beaver tried. He went even deeper, so deep that all was dark, but he could not reach the bottom either. The Loon tried, swimming with his strong wings. He was gone a long, long time, but he, too, failed to bring up Earth. Soon it seemed that all had tried and all had failed. Then a small voice spoke.

"I will bring up Earth or die trying." They looked to see who it was. It was the Tiny Muskrat. She dove down and swam and swam. She was not as strong or as swift as the others, but she was determined. She went so deep that it was all dark, and still she swam deeper. She swam so deep that her lungs felt ready to burst, but she swam deeper still. At last, just as she was becoming unconscious, she reached out one small paw and grasped at the bottom, barely touching it before she floated up, almost dead.

When the other animals saw her break the surface they thought she had failed. Then they saw her right paw was held tightly shut. "She has the Earth," they said. "Now where can we put it?"

"Place it on my back," said a deep voice. It was the Great Turtle, who had come up from the depths.
They brought the Muskrat over to the Great Turtle and placed her paw against his back. To this day there are marks at the back of the Turtle's shell which were made by the Muskrat's paw. The tiny bit of Earth fell on the back of the Turtle. Almost immediately, it began to grow larger and larger and larger until it became the whole world.

Then the two Swans brought the Sky Woman down. She stepped onto the new Earth and opened her hand, letting the seeds fall onto the bare soil. From those seeds the trees and the grass sprang up. Life on Earth had begun.

from The Navajo Origin Legend

Navajo   Retold by Washington Matthews

On the morning of the twelfth day the people washed themselves well. The women dried themselves with yellow cornmeal; the men with white cornmeal. Soon after the ablutions were completed they heard the distant call of the approaching gods. It was shouted, as before, four times – nearer and louder at each repetition – and, after the fourth call, the gods appeared. Blue Body and Black Body each carried a sacred buckskin. White Body carried two ears of corn, one yellow, one white, each covered at the end completely with grains.

The gods laid one buckskin on the ground with the head to the west: on this they placed the two ears of corn, with their tips to the east, and over the corn they spread the other buckskin with its head to the east; under the white ear they put the feather of a white eagle, under the yellow ear the feather of a yellow eagle. Then they told the people to stand at a distance and allow the wind to enter. The white wind blew from the east, and the yellow wind blew from the west, between the skins. While the wind was blowing, eight of the Mirage People came and walked around the objects on the ground four times, and as they walked the eagle feathers, whose tips protruded from between the buckskins, were seen to move. When the Mirage People had finished their walk the upper buckskin was lifted; the ears of corn had disappeared, a man and a woman lay there in their stead.

The white ear of corn had been changed into a man, the yellow ear into a woman. It was the wind that gave them life. It is the wind that comes out of our mouths now that gives us life. When this ceases to blow we die. In the skin at the tips of our fingers we see the trail of the wind; it shows us where the wind blew when our ancestors were created.

The pair thus crated were First Man and First Woman (Atse' Hastin and Atse' Estsan). The gods directed the people to build an enclosure of brushwood for the pair. When the enclosure was finished, First Man and First Woman entered it, and the gods said to them: "Live together now as husband and wife."

Journal #2: Native Myths

1. Explain what you can infer about the place of dreams in Native American Culture from the excerpt from "The Earth on Turtle's Back."
    a. Identify the main characters of this myth.
    b. What conflicts can you identify?
2. What does the excerpt from "When Grizzles Walked Upright" tell you about the beliefs of Native Americans regarding taking responsibility for one's actions?
    a. Describe the setting of this myth and possible conflicts.
3. What does the excerpt from "The Navajo Origin Legend" tell you about why the Navajo believed the wind was what gave life to people?
    a. What is the outcome of this myth?
    b. What conflicts led to this outcome?

Colonial America and the Puritans – prehistory up to 1750

This group of writings are from those who were coming to America to settle a new land. Most of the literature is comprised of letters, diaries, journals and histories. The accuracy of these writings is often called in to question Authors include Columbus, John Smith and William Bradford.

Puritanical works were written by those who were leaving Europe to find religious freedom. This society was dominated by rules and a fear of sin and as a result spending eternity in hell. Literature from this period is typically in the form of sermons, poetry, diaries and moral based stories. Themes from this time period include Religion, nature vs society, exploration, and hardship.

Authors from this period include: Anne Bradstreet, Edward Taylor and Jonathon Edwards. Examples of works during this time include: Bradford's Of Plymouth Plantation; Rowlandson's "A Narrative of the Captivity"; Edward's "Sinners in the Hands of an Angry God." Though not written during Puritan times, *The Crucible* and *The Scarlet Letter* depict life during the time when Puritan theocracy prevailed and are often read/taught during the study of this time period.

Overview of the Calvinistic Doctrine

To better understand the life in which most early colonists lived, it is beneficial to understand their religious beliefs.

According to Calvinism:
Salvation is accomplished by the almighty power of the triune God. The Father chose a people, the Son died for them, the
Holy Spirit makes Christ's death effective by bringing the elect to faith and repentance, thereby causing them to willingly obey the Gospel. determines who will be the recipients of the gift of salvation. Furthermore, the Calvinist believes that man
has no part in his own salvation; that God is supremely sovereign. If man did have a role in salvation, he would detract from the supreme power of God.

The Five Points of Calvinism
The Five Points of Calvinism are easily remembered by the acrostic **TULIP**
T-Total Depravity (Total Inability)
Total Depravity is probably the most misunderstood tenet of Calvinism.
The effect of the fall upon man is that sin has extended to every part of his personality -- his thinking, his emotions, and his will. Not necessarily that he is *intensely* sinful, but that sin has *extended* to his entire being.
U-Unconditional Election
Unconditional Election is the doctrine which states that God chose those whom he was pleased to bring to a knowledge of himself, not based upon any merit shown.
L-Limited Atonement (Particular Redemption)
The belief that Christ died to atone for specific sins of
specific sinners. Christ died to make holy the church. He did not atone for all men, because obviously all men are not saved.
I-Irresistible Grace
The result of God's Irresistible Grace is the certain response by the elect to the inward call of the Holy Spirit, when the outward call is given by the evangelist or minister of the Word of God.
P-Perseverance of the Saints
Perseverance of the Saints is a doctrine which states that the saints (those whom God has saved) will remain in God's hand until they are glorified and brought to abide with him in heaven.

Sinners in the Hands of an Angry God – Jonathan Edwards:

The following is a sermon written by British Colonial Christian theologian Jonathan Edwards, preached to his own congregation in Northampton, Massachusetts to unknown effect, and again on July 8, 1741 in Enfield, Connecticut. It is an appeal to '*sinners*' to recognize that they will be judged by *God* and that this judgment will be more fearful and painful than they can comprehend.

Deuteronomy xxxii. 35.—Their foot shall slide in due time.

In this verse is threatened the vengeance of God on the wicked unbelieving Israelites, that were God's visible people, and lived under means of grace; and that notwithstanding all God's wonderful works that he had wrought towards that people, yet remained, as is expressed verse 28, void of counsel, having no understanding in them; and that, under all the cultivations of heaven, brought forth bitter and poisonous fruit; as in the two verses next preceding the text.

The expression that I have chosen for my text, their foot shall slide in due time, seems to imply the following things relating to the punishment and destruction that these wicked Israelites were exposed to.

1. That they were always exposed to destruction; as one that stands or walks in slippery places is always exposed to fall. This is implied in the manner of their destruction's coming upon them, being represented by their foot's sliding. The same is expressed, Psalm lxxiii. 18: "Surely thou didst set them in slippery places; thou castedst them down into destruction."

2. It implies that they were always exposed to sudden, unexpected destruction; as he that walks in slippery places is every moment liable to fall, he can't foresee one moment whether he shall stand or fall the next; and when he does fall, he falls at once, without warning, which is also expressed in that Psalm lxxiii. 18, 19: "Surely thou didst set them in slippery places: thou castedst them down into destruction. How are they brought into desolation, as in a moment!"

[Pg 79]3. Another thing implied is, that they are liable to fall of themselves, without being thrown down by the hand of another; as he that stands or walks on slippery ground needs nothing but his own weight to throw him down.

4. That the reason why they are not fallen already, and don't fall now, is only that God's appointed time is not come. For it is said that when that due time, or appointed time comes, their foot shall slide. Then they shall be left to fall, as they are inclined by their own weight. God won't hold them up in these slippery places any longer, but will let them go; and then, at that very instant, they shall fall to destruction; as he that stands in such slippery declining ground on the edge of a pit that he can't stand alone, when he is let go he immediately falls and is lost.

The observation from the words that I would now insist upon is this,

There is nothing that keeps wicked men at any one moment out of hell, but the mere pleasure of God.

By the mere pleasure of God, I mean his sovereign pleasure, his arbitrary will, restrained by no obligation, hindered by no manner of difficulty, any more than if nothing else but God's mere will had in the least degree or in any respect whatsoever any hand in the preservation of wicked men one moment.

The truth of this observation may appear by the following considerations.

1. There is no want of power in God to cast wicked men into hell at any moment. Men's hands can't be strong when God rises up: the strongest have no power to resist him, nor can any deliver out of his hands.

He is not only able to cast wicked men into hell, but he can most easily do it. Sometimes an earthly prince meets with a great deal of difficulty to subdue a rebel that has found means[Pg 80] to fortify himself, and has made himself strong by the number of his followers. But it is not so with God. There is no fortress that is any defence against the power of God. Though hand join in hand, and vast multitudes of God's enemies combine and associate themselves, they are easily broken in pieces: they are as great heaps of light chaff before the whirlwind; or large quantities of dry stubble before devouring flames. We find it easy to tread on and crush a worm that we see crawling on the earth; so 'tis easy for us to cut or singe a slender thread that any thing hangs by; thus easy is it for God, when he pleases, to cast his enemies down to hell. What are we, that we should think to stand before him, at whose rebuke the earth trembles, and before whom the rocks are thrown down!

2. They deserve to be cast into hell; so that divine justice never stands in the way, it makes no objection against God's using his power at any moment to destroy them. Yea, on the contrary, justice calls aloud for an infinite punishment of their sins. Divine justice says of the tree that brings forth such grapes of Sodom, "Cut it down, why cumbereth it the ground?" Luke xiii. 7. The sword of divine justice is every moment brandished over their heads, and 'tis nothing but the hand of arbitrary mercy, and God's mere will, that holds it back.

3. They are already under a sentence of condemnation to hell. They don't only justly deserve to be cast down thither, but the sentence of the law of God, that eternal and immutable rule of righteousness that God has fixed between him and mankind, is gone out against them, and stands against them; so that they are bound over already to hell: John iii. 18, "He that believeth not is condemned already." So that every unconverted man properly belongs to hell; that is his place; from thence he is: John viii. 23, "Ye are from beneath:" and thither he is bound; 'tis the place that justice, and God's word, and the sentence of his unchangeable law, assigns to him.

They are now the objects of that very same anger and[Pg 81] wrath of God, that is expressed in the torments of hell: and the reason why they don't go down to hell at each moment is not because God, in whose power they are, is not then very angry with them; as angry as he is with many of those miserable creatures that he is now tormenting in hell, and do there feel and bear the fierceness of his wrath. Yea, God is a great deal more angry with great numbers that are now on earth, yea, doubtless, with many that are now in this congregation, that, it may be, are at ease and quiet, than he is with many of those that are now in the flames of hell.

So that it is not because God is unmindful of their wickedness, and don't resent it, that he don't let loose his hand and cut them off. God is not altogether such a one as themselves, though they may imagine him to be so. The wrath of God burns against them; their damnation don't slumber; the pit is prepared; the fire is made ready; the furnace is now hot, ready to receive them; the flames do now rage and glow. The glittering sword is whet, and held over them, and the pit hath opened her mouth under them.

5. The devil stands ready to fall upon them, and seize them as his own, at what moment God shall permit him. They belong to him; he has their souls in his possession, and under his dominion. The Scripture represents them as his goods, Luke xi. 21. The devils watch them; they are ever by them, at their right hand; they stand waiting for them, like greedy hungry lions that see their prey, and expect to have it, but are for the present kept back; if God should withdraw his hand by which they are restrained, they would in one moment fly upon their poor souls. The old serpent is gaping for them; hell opens its mouth wide to receive them; and if God should permit it, they would be hastily swallowed up and lost.

6. There are in the souls of wicked men those hellish principles reigning, that would presently kindle and flame out into hell-fire, if it were not for God's restraints. There is laid in[Pg 82] the very nature of carnal men a foundation for the torments of hell: there are those corrupt principles, in reigning power in them, and in full possession of them, that are seeds of hell-fire. These principles are active and powerful, exceeding violent in their nature, and if it were not for the restraining hand of God upon them, they would soon break out, they would flame out after the same manner as the same corruptions, the same enmity does in the heart of damned souls, and would beget the same torments in 'em as they do in them. The souls of the wicked are in Scripture compared to the troubled sea, Isaiah lvii. 20. For the present God restrains their wickedness by his mighty power, as he does the raging waves of the troubled sea, saying, "Hitherto shalt thou come, and no further;" but if God should withdraw that restraining power, it would soon carry all afore it. Sin is the ruin and misery of the soul; it is destructive in its nature; and if God should leave it without restraint, there would need nothing else to make the soul perfectly miserable. The corruption of the heart of man is a thing that is immoderate and boundless in its fury; and while wicked men live here, it is like fire pent up by God's restraints, whenas if it were let loose, it would set on fire the course of nature; and as the heart is now a sink of sin, so, if sin was not restrained, it would immediately turn the soul into a fiery oven, or a furnace of fire and brimstone.

7. It is no security to wicked men for one moment, that there are no visible means of death at hand. 'Tis no security to a natural man, that he is now in health, and that he don't see which way he should now immediately go out of the world by any accident, and that there is no visible danger in any respect in his circumstances. The manifold and continual experience of the world in all ages shows that this is no evidence that a man is not on the very brink of eternity, and that the next step won't be into another world. The unseen, unthought of ways and means of persons' going suddenly out of[Pg 83] the world are innumerable and inconceivable. Unconverted men walk over the pit of hell on a rotten covering, and there are innumerable places in this covering so weak that they won't bear their weight, and these places are not

seen. The arrows of death fly unseen at noonday; the sharpest sight can't discern them. God has so many different, unsearchable ways of taking wicked men out of the world and sending 'em to hell, that there is nothing to make it appear that God had need to be at the expense of a miracle, or go out of the ordinary course of his providence, to destroy any wicked man, at any moment. All the means that there are of sinners' going out of the world are so in God's hands, and so absolutely subject to his power and determination, that it don't depend at all less on the mere will of God, whether sinners shall at any moment go to hell, than if means were never made use of, or at all concerned in the case.

8. Natural men's prudence and care to preserve their own lives, or the care of others to preserve them, don't secure 'em a moment. This, divine providence and universal experience does also bear testimony to. There is this clear evidence that men's own wisdom is no security to them from death; that if it were otherwise we should see some difference between the wise and politic men of the world and others, with regard to their liableness to early and unexpected death; but how is it in fact? Eccles. ii. 16, "How dieth the wise man? As the fool."

9. All wicked men's pains and contrivance they use to escape hell, while they continue to reject Christ, and so remain wicked men, don't secure 'em from hell one moment. Almost every natural man that hears of hell flatters himself that he shall escape it; he depends upon himself for his own security, he flatters himself in what he has done, in what he is now doing, or what he intends to do; every one lays out matters in his own mind how he shall avoid damnation, and flatters [Pg 84]himself that he contrives well for himself, and that his schemes won't fail. They hear indeed that there are but few saved, and that the bigger part of men that have died heretofore are gone to hell; but each one imagines that he lays out matters better for his own escape than others have done: he don't intend to come to that place of torment; he says within himself, that he intends to take care that shall be effectual, and to order matters so for himself as not to fail.

But the foolish children of men do miserably delude themselves in their own schemes, and in their confidence in their own strength and wisdom; they trust to nothing but a shadow. The bigger part of those that heretofore have lived under the same means of grace, and are now dead, are undoubtedly gone to hell; and it was not because they were not as wise as those that are now alive; it was not because they did not lay out matters as well for themselves to secure their own escape. If it were so that we could come to speak with them, and could inquire of them, one by one, whether they expected, when alive, and when they used to hear about hell, ever to be subjects of that misery, we, doubtless, should hear one and another reply, "No, I never intended to come here: I had laid out matters otherwise in my mind; I thought I should contrive well for myself: I thought my scheme good: I intended to take effectual care; but it came upon me unexpected; I did not look for it at that time, and in that manner; it came as a thief: death outwitted me: God's wrath was too quick for me. O my cursed foolishness! I was flattering myself, and pleasing myself with vain dreams of what I would do hereafter; and when I was saying peace and safety, then sudden destruction came upon me."

10. God has laid himself under no obligation, by any promise, to keep any natural man out of hell one moment. God certainly has made no promises either of eternal life, or of any deliverance or preservation from eternal death, but what are contained in the covenant of grace, the promises that are given[Pg 85] in Christ, in whom all the promises are yea and amen. But surely they have no interest in the promises of the covenant of grace that are not the children of the covenant, and that do not believe in any of the promises of the covenant, and have no interest in the Mediator of the covenant.

So that, whatever some have imagined and pretended about promises made to natural men's earnest seeking and knocking, 'tis plain and manifest, that whatever pains a natural man takes in religion, whatever prayers he makes, till he believes in Christ, God is under no manner of obligation to keep him a moment from eternal destruction.

So that thus it is, that natural men are held in the hand of God over the pit of hell; they have deserved the fiery pit, and are already sentenced to it; and God is dreadfully provoked, his anger is as great towards them as to those that are actually suffering the executions of the fierceness of his wrath in hell, and they have done nothing in the least to appease or abate that anger, neither is God in the least bound by any promise to hold 'em up one moment; the devil is waiting for them, hell is gaping for them, the flames gather and flash about them, and would fain lay hold on them and swallow them up; the fire pent up in their own hearts is struggling to break out; and they have no interest in any Mediator, there are no means within reach that can be any security to them. In short they have no refuge, nothing to take hold of; all that preserves them every moment is the mere arbitrary will, and uncovenanted, unobliged forbearance of an incensed God.

Journal # 3:

1. Consider your prior knowledge of Puritan life and belief systems. In what ways does Edwards' sermon model Puritan beliefs?
2. What are the prominent themes communicated by the images and analogies that Edwards uses?
3. This sermon is illustrating the biblical concept of sin being a great grievance against God that must be punished. There is a turning point in this sermon which begins with, "And now you have an extraordinary opportunity, a day where Christ has thrown the door of mercy wide open, and stands calling. . ." We can look at this sermon for the religious teaching that it was, but we can also examine it for the literary piece that it was.
4. How does Edwards use rhetorical elements in the sermon? Use the devices worksheet in this text to help you identify the devices used in the sermon.

Anne Bradstreet: To my Dear and Loving Husband

She was the first North American to publish a book of poems, the first Woman and the first Puritan in North America to publish! Born and educated in England, Anne Bradstreet was the daughter of an earl's estate manager. Anne married Simon Bradstreet when she was just 16! Two years later she and her husband left Europe and moved to the Massachusetts Bay Colony. Her writing is characterized by the Puritan Plain Style *(short words, direct statements, and references to ordinary, everyday objects and events).*

The Tenth Muse was the first book of poetry published by someone living in the New World, giving her the unique distinction of being America's first poet. *The Tenth Muse* was Bradstreet's only publication during her lifetime. After her death in 1672, a second edition was printed --"To My Dear and Loving Husband" first appeared in this second edition, which came off the presses in 1678.

If ever two were one, then surely we.
If ever man were loved by wife, then thee.
If ever wife was happy in a man,
Compare with me, ye women, if you can.
I prize thy love more than whole mines of gold,
Or all the riches that the East doth hold.
My love is such that rivers cannot quench,
Nor ought but love from thee give recompense.
Thy love is such I can no way repay;
The heavens reward thee manifold, I pray.
Then while we live, in love let's so persever,
That when we live no more, we may live ever.

Anne Bradstreet Journal #4:
1. What are some examples of plain language in the poem?
2. Why do you think she uses this type of language?
3. What examples of language in the poem show more dynamic language usage? Why does it seem to stand out?
4. Using the Devices worksheet, identify some of the devices she uses in her poem.

Essay Assignment #1: Novel Essay

A word on Plagiarism

If your paper plagiarizes any writer's work--no matter to what degree--it will receive a zero. Plagiarism means that you have taken an idea from another writer without showing attribution, even if you have paraphrased it in your own words. Any words or ideas taken from other writers must be attributed with a citation.

Essay Assignment:

on one text. *Plan for only two – three body paragraphs* – 4—5 paragraphs total. Choose from the set of topics below. Each body paragraph will require at least two quotations from the text properly embedded and properly cited according to MLA citation. Plan on one explanatory sentence for each quote. Construct a cogent paper from thesis to topic sentences and provide close analysis of text. Use the Basic Essay Outline and the thesis information on the next two pages for this and future essays.

The writing process—drafting, re-drafting and editing—

1) **the thesis and topic sentences** --use a scratch outline/notes to generate these.
2) Then, work on a **2) first draft** of 1.5-2 pages minimum, shown it to me by the week the paper is due, and then;
3) **3) final draft** (of 2-3 pages).

Grading Criteria

- Substantive points for thesis and topic sentences; and
- Close/detailed/precise analysis of the text (use at least three quotations and analyze them closely).
- Literary-historical context in the introduction paragraph and, when appropriate, throughout.
- If appropriate, include a discussion of how the issue, quote, theme, or text can be explained within a Biblical context – use 1-2 Biblical quotes, explained, in your paper for full analysis.

As you choose one of the topics below, be sure to frame your argument based on that topic as it can be shown as a commentary on the nature of American literature in general. Thus you'll be formulating a theory of American literature from the basis of your close analysis of that text.

Hawthorne's *The Scarlet Letter*

1. Projection onto nature. Hawthorne recognized the power of nature as a space on which to construct his ideas of human freedom. Examine the nature scenes in the novel and speculate on what kind of image Hawthorne creates of it. Develop a theory as to what he constructs of nature and what function it serves in addressing one of the themes of the novel (especially freedom versus constraint).

2. Symbolism: The novel makes extensive use of symbols. Discuss the difference between the Puritans" use of symbols (the meteor, for example) and the way that the narrator makes use of symbols. Do both have religious implications? Do symbols foreshadow events or simply comment on them after the fact? How do they help the characters understand their lives, and how do they help the reader understand Hawthorne's book?

3. The nature of sin: Do guilt and blame work together to bring reformation of any of the characters in this book? Why or why not? Can you have guilt without blame, or blame without guilt?   What does "redemption" mean to the Puritans in this novel? What does "redemption" seem to mean in the text and for the other characters—to Chillingworth, Dimmesdale, and Pearl?   According to The Scarlet Letter, does redemption require confession? To whom?

4. Hypocrisy: Hypocrisy is sometimes necessary. Dimmesdale destroys himself through hypocrisy, but his life is a blessing to many in the community. Even though hypocrisy appears to save Dimmesdale from punishment and humiliation, his torment is worse even than Hester's. Which characters are represented as hypocrites in this book and why? Who is free of hypocrisy, and why? Is the community itself hypocritical?   Where does hypocrisy seem to rank on the Puritan Sin Hierarchy? Is it possible to say that Hester Prynne is a hypocrite? Why or why not?

Basic Essay Outline

Overview of topic

Introduction Paragraph:

Main Idea of the Paper: _____

Argument 1: _____

Argument 2: _____

Argument 3: _____

Thesis in one sentence: _____

_____

Body Paragraph 1:

Restate Argument 1: _____

Reason 1: _____

Quote 1 _____

Reason 3: _____

Conclusion Sentence: _____

_____

Body Paragraph 2:

Restate Argument 2: _____

Reason 1: _____

Quote 2 _____

Reason 3: _____

Conclusion Sentence: _____

_____

Body Paragraph 3:

Restate Argument 3: _____

Reason 1: _____

Quote 3 _____

Reason 3: _____

Conclusion Sentence: _____

_____

Conclusion:

Main Idea Rephrased: _____

Rephrase Argument 1: _____

Rephrase Argument 2: _____

Rephrase Argument 3: _____

Conclusion Sentence: _____

_____

Writing Your Thesis

Use this information to help you write your essays

WHAT A THESIS STATEMENT SHOULD NOT BE:

1. A topic or subject by itself cannot serve as a thesis statement. That information tells what the paper is about, but not what you and your research have to say about it.
2. A question cannot serve as a thesis statement because it is not a statement. A question merely says that an answer will follow. However, a question-and-answer pair can be a thesis statement.
3. A general statement that lacks a detailed point of view cannot serve as a thesis statement. A general statement may give the reader background information but does not reflect your point of view.
4. A "so what?" statement. This kind of thesis statement is too obvious (common knowledge) and demonstrates no originality of thought.

WHAT A THESIS STATEMENT SHOULD BE:

1. A complete sentence or two summarizing the point of view in your paper as prompted by the assignment.
2. A specific declaration of your main idea about the prompt.
3. A statement reflecting **your position** about the prompt – establish this by answer the questions in the prompt with what YOU think about those ideas.

EXAMPLES:

THESIS: *The Midwife's Apprentice* is a realistic interpretation of the Middle Ages, showing what life was really like for the common villager.

THESIS: Throughout *To Kill A Mockingbird* we see Scout Finch mature as she becomes aware of the true nature of the people in her town.

<u>American Enlightenment – 1750 – 1800</u>

Also known as Rationalism/Classicism and The Age of Reason. Best known for political and philosophical writings focusing on reason and common sense. These writings contributed, in part, to the American Revolution. Authors of this period include Benjamin Franklin, Thomas Jefferson, Thomas Paine, Patrick Henry and Phillis Wheatly. The writing was intended to tell readers how to interpret what they are reading, encourage Revolutionary War support, and instruct in values.

The genre and style of the time included: Political pamphlets, travel writing, a highly ornate style, and persuasive writing. These writings effectively grew patriotism, Instilled pride, created common agreement about issues, and crafted a national mission and American character.

Common Sense – Thomas Paine

Paine wrote mostly pamphlets that would spur ideas and immediate action. In the document "The American Crisis," Paine wrote about the oppression that America suffered from Britain, and propelled America into a war with Britain.

In December 1776, Thomas Paine, the author of the sensational pamphlet *Common Sense*, published *The Crisis, No. 1*, the first of a series of pamphlets he wrote during the next seven years. In the following excerpts from that broadside, what are the primary arguments Paine puts forth for the Patriot cause? What is most and least persuasive in his arguments?

THESE are the times that try men's souls: The summer soldier and the sunshine patriot will, in this crisis, shrink from the service of his country but he that stands it NOW, deserves the love and thanks of man and woman. Tyranny, like hell, is not easily conquered; yet we have this consolation with us, that the harder the conflict, the more glorious the triumph. What we obtain, too cheap, we esteem too lightly:--'Tis dearness only that gives every thing its value. <u>Heaven</u> knows how to set a proper price upon its goods; and it would be strange indeed, if so celestial an article as Freedom should not be highly rated. Britain, with an army to enforce her tyranny, has declared, that she has a right (not only to TAX) but "to BIND us in ALL CASES WHATSOEVER," and if being bound in that manner is not slavery, then is there not such a thing as slavery upon earth. Even the expression is impious, for so unlimited a power can belong only to God.

Whether the Independence of the Continent was declared too soon, or delayed too long, I will not now enter into as an argument; my own simple opinion in that had it been eight months earlier, it would have been much better. We did not make a proper use of last winter, neither could we while we were in a dependent state. However, the fault, if it were one, was all our own; we have none to blame but ourselves. But no great deal is lost yet; all that Howe has been doing for this month past is rather a ravage than a conquered which the spirit of the Jersies a year ago would have quickly repulsed, and which time and a little resolution with soon recover. . . .

I shall not now attempt to give all the particulars of our retreat [through New Jersey] to the Delaware [River], suffice it for the present to say, that both officers and men, though greatly harassed and fatigued, frequently without self, covering or provision, the inevitable consequences of a long retreat, bore it with a manly and martial spirit. All their wishes were one, which was, that the country would turn out and help them to drive the enemy back. Voltaire has remarked, that king William never appeared to full advantage but in difficulties and in action; the same remark may be made on General Washington for the character fits him. There is a natural fannels in some minds which cannot be unlocked by trifles, but which, when unlocked discovers a cabinet of fortitude, and I reckon it among those kind of public blessing, which we do not immediately see, that God hath blest him with uninterrupted health, and gives him a mind that can even flourish upon care.

I shall conclude this paper with some miscellaneous remarks on the slate of our affairs; and shall begin with asking the following question, Why is it that the enemy hath left the New England provinces, and made those middle once the fear of war? The answer is easy, New England is not infested with Tories, and we are. I have been under in raising the cry against these men, and used numberless arguments to shew them their danger. . . . The period is now arrived, in which either they or we must change our sentiments, or one or both must fall. And what is a Tory? Good GOD! what is he? I should not be afraid to go with a hundred Whigs against a thousand Tories, were they to attempt to get into arms. Every Tory is a coward, for a servile, slavish, self-interested fear is the foundation of Toryism; and a man under such influence, though he may be cruel, never can be brave.

But before the line of irrecoverable separation be drawn between us, let us reason the matter together: Your conduct is an invitation to the enemy, yet not one in a thousand of you has heart enough to join him. Howe is as much deceived by you as the American cause is injured by you. He expects you will all take up arms, and flock to his standard with muskets on your shoulders, Your opinions are of no use to him, unless you support him personally; for 'tis soldiers, and not Tories, that he wants. . . .

Quitting this class of men [i.e., Tories], I turn with the warm ardour of a friend to those who have nobly stood yet determined to stand the matter out; I call not upon a few, but upon all; not on THIS state or THAT truth but on EVERY state; up and help us; lay your shoulders to the wheel; better have too much force than too little, when so great an object is at stake. Let it be told to the future world, that in the depth of winter, when nothing but hope and virtue could survive, that the city and the country, alarmed at one common danger, come forth to meet and to repulse it. Say not, that thousands are gone, turn out your tens of thousands; throw not the bur hen of the day upon Providence, but "Shew your faith by your works," that God may bless you. It matters not where you live, or what rank of life you hold, the evil or the blessing will reach you all. The far and the near, the home counties and the back, the rich and the poor, shall suffer or rejoice alike. The heart that feels not now, is dead: The blood of his children shall curse his cowardice, who shrinks back at a time when a little might have saved the whole, and made them happy. I love the man that can smile in trouble, that can gather strength from distress, and grow brave by reflection. 'Tis the business of little minds to shrink; but he whose heart is firm, and whose conscience approves his conduct, will pursue his principles unto death.

My own line of reasoning is to myself as strait and clear as a ray of light. Not all the treasures of the world, is far as I believe, could have induced me to support an offensive war, for I think it murder; But if a thief break into my house, burn and destroy my property, and kill or threaten to kill me, or those that are in it, and to "bind me in all cases whatsoever," to his absolute will, am I to suffer it? What signifies it to me, whether he who does it, is a king or a common man; my countryman or not my countryman; whether it is done by an individual villain, or an army of them? If we reason to the root of things we shall find no difference; neither can any just cause be assigned why we should punish in the one case, and pardon in the other. Let them call me rebel, and welcome, I feel no concern from it; but I should suffer the misery of devils, were I to make a whore of my soul by swearing allegiance to one, whose character is that of a stupid, stubborn, worthless, brutish man. I conceive likewise a horrid idea in receiving mercy from a being, who as the last day shall be shrieking to the rocks and mountains to cover him, and fleeing with terror from the orphan, the widow and the slain of America. . . .

I thank God that I fear not. I see no real cause for fear. I know one situation well, and can see the way out of it. While our army was collected, Howe dared not risk a battle, and it is not credit to him that he decamped from the White Plains, and waited a mean opportunity to ravage the defenceless Jersies; but it is great credit to us, that, with an handful of men, we sustained an orderly retreat for near an hundred miles, brought off our ammunition, all our field pieces, the greatest part of our stores, and had four rivers to pass. None can say that our retreat was precipitate, for we were near three weeks in performing it, that the country might have time to come in. Twice we marched back to meet the enemy and remained out till dark. The sign of fear was not seen in our camp, and had not some of the cowardly and disaffected inhabitants spread false alarms through the country, the Jersies had never been ravaged. Once more we are again collected and collecting; our new army at both ends of the continent recruiting fast, and we shall be able to open the next campaign with sixty thousand men; well armed & cloathed. This is our situation, and who will may know it. By perseverance and fortitude have the prospect of a glorious issue, by cowardice and the sad choice of a variety of evils-- a ravaged country--a depopulated city--habituations without safety, and slavery without hope--our homes turned into barracks . . . .

Journal #5 Thomas Paine

Persuasion tries to convince reader to accept a specific viewpoint of an issue and perhaps take action. A good persuasive writing uses a combination of logical and emotional appeals to thoroughly persuade the audience.

A logical appeal uses a chain of reasoning to establish the validity of an argument. We refer to this as *logos*. With logic, the arguer moves from either a general premise to a specific conclusion, or uses specific premises to arrive at a general conclusion. Example: "Britain, with an army to enforce her tyranny, has declared, that she has a right (not only to TAX) but "to BIND us in ALL CASES WHATSOEVER," and if being bound in that manner is not slavery, then is there not such a thing as slavery upon earth."

An emotional appeal seeks to stir the reader's feelings. We refer to this as *pathos*. It relies more on charged words or symbolic language to evoke sympathy or distaste. Example: "The heart that feels not now, is dead: The blood of his children shall curse his cowardice, who shrinks back at a time when a little might have saved the whole, and made them happy."

Part ONE: Identify the type(s) of appeal used and the effect he hopes it will have on his audience:

1. Tyranny, like hell, is not easily conquered; yet we have this consolation with us, that the harder the conflict, the more glorious the triumph. What we obtain, too cheap, we esteem too lightly:--'Tis dearness only that gives every thing its value.

2. I turn with the warm ardour of a friend to those who have nobly stood yet determined to stand the matter out; I call not upon a few, but upon all; not on THIS state or THAT truth but on EVERY state;

3. Not all the treasures of the world, is far as I believe, could have induced me to support an offensive war, for I think it murder; But if a thief break into my house, burn and destroy my property, and kill or threaten to kill me, or those that are in it, and to "bind me in all cases whatsoever," to his absolute will, am I to suffer it? What signifies it to me, whether he who does it, is a king or a common man; my countryman or not my countryman; whether it is done by an individual villain, or an army of them? If we reason to the root of things we shall find no difference; neither can any just cause be assigned why we should punish in the one case, and pardon in the other

Part TWO:

1. Give Background on the argument: what information does Paine provide?
2. How does he deal with panic?
3. How does he glorify Washington?
4. How does he attack Tories and sympathizers?
5. Look back at the passages and identify any "charged" language- any words or language that is used solely to elicit a strong emotional response from the reader, or words that have an association that can affect the reader. Then, using the Devices worksheet, identify rhetorical devices Paine uses in his writing.

Journal #6 – Kipling:

Read the following Poem by British author Rudyard Kipling about the American Revolution.

The American Rebellion

Twas not while England's sword unsheathed
    Put half a world to flight,
  Nor while their new-built cities breathed
    Secure behind her might;
Not while she poured from Pole to Line
    Treasure and ships and men--
These worshippers at Freedoms shrine
    They did not quit her then!

Not till their foes were driven forth
    By England o'er the main--
Not till the Frenchman from the North
    Had gone with shattered Spain;
Not till the clean-swept oceans showed
    No hostile flag unrolled,
Did they remember that they owed
    To Freedom--and were bold!

Answer the following question in a short paragraph:

What is Kipling's point of view about the American Revolution in this part of the poem? Cite specific examples. Make a comment about why you think the poem is titled the way it is.

Unit 2 - Romanticism 1820 – 1860

The Romantic era was a continuation of the same movement in Europe. It was marked by authors who focused on individualism, idealism, imagination and nature. Often set their works in distant times or places. This is the first movement to really produce a body of work that embodied the idea of America, its raw, natural setting and its broad landscapes, while rebelling against the Classicism movement. Not surprisingly, this is the largest body of work to this point in history and one that we spend a lot of time studying.

After the "Age of Reason" came to an end, the people of America were tired of reality; they wanted to see life as more than it was. Struggling to make sense of their complex, inconsistent society, writers of the period turned inward for a sense of truth. Their movement, known as romanticism, explored the glories of the individual spirit, the beauty of nature, and the possibilities of the imagination. This was **the Era of Romantics**. The main medium that presented itself at that time were short stories, poems, and novels. During this era, as appose to the "Age of Reason" the imagination dominated; intuition ruled over fact. Authors in the Romantic Era include Washington Irving, Edgar Allen Poe, Nathaniel Hawthorne (which we read with the Scarlet Letter), James Fenimore Cooper, Emily Dickenson, and Herman Melville.

Historical constructs during this time include: Expansion of magazines, newspapers, and book publishing, slavery debates, and industrial revolution that brought ideas that the "old ways" of doing things which were now irrelevant. Aspects of Romanticism focused on valuing feeling and intuition over reasoning, journeying away from corruption of civilization and limits of rational thought toward the integrity of nature and freedom of the imagination, helping instill proper gender behavior for men and women, and allowing people to re-imagine the American past.

Writers of the romantic period were witness to a period of great growth and opportunity for the young American nation with **westward expansion**. Toward the middle of the century, Americans embraced the notion of "manifest destiny"— the ideas that it was the destiny of the United States to expand to the Pacific Ocean and into Mexican territory. When the War of 1812 interrupted trade with the British, Americans were suddenly forced to produce many of the goods they had previously imported. **The Industrial Revolution** began, changing the country from a largely agrarian economy to an industrial powerhouse.

Ralph Waldo Emerson led a group practicing **transcendentalism**—a philosophical and literary movement that emphasized living a simple life and celebrating the truth found in personal emotion and imagination. Exalting the dignity of the individual, the transcendentalist stressed American ideas of optimism, freedom, and self-reliance.

Gothic literature was a genre also introduced at this time, which is a sub-genre of Romanticism, this genre included stories about characters that had both good and evil traits. Gothic literature also incorporated to use of supernatural elements, mystery, and darker settings. Other genres include: character sketches, frontier exploits, slave narratives, poetry, short stories, and dark romanticism/light romanticism.

Washington Irving – The Legend of Sleepy Hollow

Irving (1783-1859) was the first "famous" American author; he's also known as the "Father of American Literature." He wrote travel books, short stories, and satires, and was one of the first American authors to earn acclaim in Europe. He advocated for writing as a legitimate profession and argued for stronger laws to protect American writers from copyright infringement. Some of his works include; *Legend of Sleepy Hollow, Rip Van Winkle*, and Devil and *Tom Walker*. Use the link in the introduction to access the short story, *The Legend of Sleepy Hollow*, published in 1820.

Journal #7 - Irving:

1. What mood does the setting of this story create?
2. Who do the villagers believe the headless horseman is? How did he lose his head?
3. What do the villagers think he is doing out at night? Why is he said to be in such a hurry?
4. Where does Ichabod Crane live? Why does he need to be able to have all of his belongings in a small bundle?
5. Why do the women in the countryside think he is an important person? How do the mothers treat him as a result? How do the younger girls respond to him?
6. What approach does Brom Bones (Brom Van Brunt) want to take when he discovers Ichabod is interested in Katrina? Why can't he do that?
7. Contrast Ichabod Crane and Brom Bones. How are they different in physical appearance? How are their actions different? What would have made Katrina attracted to each of them?
8. What are two things Brom Bones does to get back at Ichabod for trying to steal Katrina?
9. What evidence is there that Ichabod Crane had an active imagination?
10. What mood is Ichabod in when he leaves Katrina's house that night? What evidence is there of his mood? What speculation does the author make as to what happened?
11. What logical explanation is there for three of the things Ichabod sees or hears when he is near the old, large tree?
12. When Ichabod sees something huge and black by the brook, why doesn't he turn and run away? What two things does he do instead? What four traces of the chase do the searchers find the next day?
13. What makes it seem that Brom Bones knew something about what happened that night?
14. What did the people of the town believe about what happened that night?

The Raven   By Edgar Allan Poe

Edgar Allan Poe (1809-1849) was a southerner with a darkly metaphysical vision mixed with elements of realism, parody, and burlesque (caricature or parody). He refined the short story genre and created detective fiction. Many of his stories foreshadow the genres of science fiction, horror, and fantasy so popular today.

First published in January 1845, the poem "The Raven" is often noted for its musicality, stylized language, and supernatural atmosphere. It tells of a talking raven's mysterious visit to a distraught lover, tracing the man's slow fall into madness. "The Raven," as well as many of Poe's tales, is written backwards. The effect is determined first, and the whole plot is set; then the web grows backwards from that single effect. Poe chose Beauty to be the theme of the poem, and after choosing Beauty as the province, Poe considered sadness to be the highest manifestation of beauty.

> Once upon a midnight dreary, while I pondered, weak and weary,
> Over many a quaint and curious volume of forgotten lore—
> While I nodded, nearly napping, suddenly there came a tapping,
> As of some one gently rapping, rapping at my chamber door.
> "'Tis some visitor," I muttered, "tapping at my chamber door—
> Only this and nothing more."
>
> Ah, distinctly I remember it was in the bleak December;
> And each separate dying ember wrought its ghost upon the floor.
> Eagerly I wished the morrow;—vainly I had sought to borrow
> From my books surcease of sorrow—sorrow for the lost Lenore—
> For the rare and radiant maiden whom the angels name Lenore—
> Nameless here for evermore.
>
> And the silken, sad, uncertain rustling of each purple curtain
> Thrilled me—filled me with fantastic terrors never felt before;
> So that now, to still the beating of my heart, I stood repeating

"'Tis some visitor entreating entrance at my chamber door—
Some late visitor entreating entrance at my chamber door;—
This it is and nothing more."

Presently my soul grew stronger; hesitating then no longer,
"Sir," said I, "or Madam, truly your forgiveness I implore;
But the fact is I was napping, and so gently you came rapping,
And so faintly you came tapping, tapping at my chamber door,
That I scarce was sure I heard you"—here I opened wide the door;—
Darkness there and nothing more.

Deep into that darkness peering, long I stood there wondering, fearing,
Doubting, dreaming dreams no mortal ever dared to dream before;
But the silence was unbroken, and the stillness gave no token,
And the only word there spoken was the whispered word, "Lenore?"
This I whispered, and an echo murmured back the word, "Lenore!"—
Merely this and nothing more.

Back into the chamber turning, all my soul within me burning,
Soon again I heard a tapping somewhat louder than before.
"Surely," said I, "surely that is something at my window lattice;
Let me see, then, what thereat is, and this mystery explore—
Let my heart be still a moment and this mystery explore;—
'Tis the wind and nothing more!"

Open here I flung the shutter, when, with many a flirt and flutter,
In there stepped a stately Raven of the saintly days of yore;
Not the least obeisance made he; not a minute stopped or stayed he;
But, with mien of lord or lady, perched above my chamber door—
Perched upon a bust of Pallas just above my chamber door—
Perched, and sat, and nothing more.

Then this ebony bird beguiling my sad fancy into smiling,
By the grave and stern decorum of the countenance it wore,
"Though thy crest be shorn and shaven, thou," I said, "art sure no craven,
Ghastly grim and ancient Raven wandering from the Nightly shore—
Tell me what thy lordly name is on the Night's Plutonian shore!"
Quoth the Raven "Nevermore."

Much I marvelled this ungainly fowl to hear discourse so plainly,
Though its answer little meaning—little relevancy bore;
For we cannot help agreeing that no living human being
Ever yet was blessed with seeing bird above his chamber door—
Bird or beast upon the sculptured bust above his chamber door,
With such name as "Nevermore."

But the Raven, sitting lonely on the placid bust, spoke only
That one word, as if his soul in that one word he did outpour.
Nothing farther then he uttered—not a feather then he fluttered—
Till I scarcely more than muttered "Other friends have flown before—
On the morrow he will leave me, as my Hopes have flown before."
Then the bird said "Nevermore."

Startled at the stillness broken by reply so aptly spoken,
"Doubtless," said I, "what it utters is its only stock and store
Caught from some unhappy master whom unmerciful Disaster
Followed fast and followed faster till his songs one burden bore—

Till the dirges of his Hope that melancholy burden bore
Of 'Never—nevermore'."

But the Raven still beguiling all my fancy into smiling,
Straight I wheeled a cushioned seat in front of bird, and bust and door;
Then, upon the velvet sinking, I betook myself to linking
Fancy unto fancy, thinking what this ominous bird of yore—
What this grim, ungainly, ghastly, gaunt, and ominous bird of yore
Meant in croaking "Nevermore."

This I sat engaged in guessing, but no syllable expressing
To the fowl whose fiery eyes now burned into my bosom's core;
This and more I sat divining, with my head at ease reclining
On the cushion's velvet lining that the lamp-light gloated o'er,
But whose velvet-violet lining with the lamp-light gloating o'er,
She shall press, ah, nevermore!

Then, methought, the air grew denser, perfumed from an unseen censer
Swung by Seraphim whose foot-falls tinkled on the tufted floor.
"Wretch," I cried, "thy God hath lent thee—by these angels he hath sent thee
Respite—respite and nepenthe from thy memories of Lenore;
Quaff, oh quaff this kind nepenthe and forget this lost Lenore!"
Quoth the Raven "Nevermore."

"Prophet!" said I, "thing of evil!—prophet still, if bird or devil!—
Whether Tempter sent, or whether tempest tossed thee here ashore,
Desolate yet all undaunted, on this desert land enchanted—
On this home by Horror haunted—tell me truly, I implore—
Is there—is there balm in Gilead?—tell me—tell me, I implore!"
Quoth the Raven "Nevermore."

"Prophet!" said I, "thing of evil!—prophet still, if bird or devil!
By that Heaven that bends above us—by that God we both adore—
Tell this soul with sorrow laden if, within the distant Aidenn,
It shall clasp a sainted maiden whom the angels name Lenore—
Clasp a rare and radiant maiden whom the angels name Lenore."
Quoth the Raven "Nevermore."

"Be that word our sign of parting, bird or fiend!" I shrieked, upstarting—
"Get thee back into the tempest and the Night's Plutonian shore!
Leave no black plume as a token of that lie thy soul hath spoken!
Leave my loneliness unbroken!—quit the bust above my door!
Take thy beak from out my heart, and take thy form from off my door!"
Quoth the Raven "Nevermore."

And the Raven, never flitting, still is sitting, still is sitting
On the pallid bust of Pallas just above my chamber door;
And his eyes have all the seeming of a demon's that is dreaming,
And the lamp-light o'er him streaming throws his shadow on the floor;
And my soul from out that shadow that lies floating on the floor
Shall be lifted—nevermore!

Journal #8 – The Raven

"The Raven" is about a man and his encounter with a raven, an ominous looking bird made more terrifying by the uneasy mental condition of the poem's speaker. Work on this Journal with your instructor and on your own as homework

Stanza 1.
1. What was the speaker doing? What condition was he in?
2. What did he hear?

Stanza 2.
1. What does the speaker give us to see in the second line? What is the speaker wishing for?
2. What had he been doing? With his books? Why?
3. How was he feeling? Why?
4. Who is Lenore?
5. What does the last line mean?

Stanza 3.
1. What vision does the speaker give in the first line? How does he make it seem eerie?
2. What does he say in the second line? What seems to be happening to him?
3. What type of state does he seem to be going into? Why?

Stanza 4.
1. Does he open the door before or after he speaks?
2. What does he find when he opens the door?

Stanza 5.
1. Does he close the door or keep it open? What does he see?
2. What is the darkness like? How does it make him feel? What does he say?
3. What does he hear? Does he really hear something or is it his imagination?

Stanza 6.
1. He has shut the door and moved to the window, how does he open the window?
2. What does he find?
3. What do you know about Ravens? How does the speaker say the Raven acted in lines three and four?
4. What does the Raven do?

Stanza 7.
1. What does the bird do for the speaker in the first line? Knowing what you know about Ravens, how is this ironic?
2. Where does the speaker think the bird has come from? Why?
3. What does the speaker ask the bird? What does the bird reply?

Stanza 8.
1. How does the speaker feel about the Raven in his chamber?
2. Does he think that the bird's presence has any significance? Why/why not?

Stanza 9
1. Has the Raven moved since entering the house? How do you know (L.1 and L.3.)?
2. What does the speaker believe the bird will do?
3. When does he believe that the bird will leave? What does the bird say?

Stanza 10
1. What word does the speaker wish to be the last spoken between him and the bird?
2. Where does he tell the bird to go?
3. What is a black plume?
4. What does the speaker imply when he tells the Raven to take its beak from his heart? How does the speaker feel about the Raven at this point?

Stanza 11.
1. In the last stanza, where is the bird? What eerie vision does the speaker give in lines three & four?
2. When else in the poem did he speak of shadows?
3. Who or what might the Raven symbolize?
4. What does it mean when the speaker says that the shadow on the floor shall be lifted nevermore? (He will always carry his guilt/mourning.)
5. Who says nevermore?
6. What conclusions can we draw about what effects the Raven has had on the speaker?

Review and Conclusion questions:

1. Why did Poe use a Raven instead of another bird? What is the symbol of a Raven?
2. When did the speaker become paranoid? Why?
3. What movies/TV programs can you think of when a person becomes scared of something outside?
4. Why would Lenore be at his door if she died? How do you think she died?
5. Where does the speaker's imagination take control of his mind?

Fireside Poets:

These poets wanted to prove that American poets were as capable and sophisticated as European poets. They proved this by copying European literary traditions, and used English themes, meter and imagery. Who were the Fireside Poets? Henry Wadsworth Longfellow, John Greenleaf Whittier, Oliver Wendell Holmes, and James Russell Lowell.

Traditionalists who relied on past literary forms Subject Matter of Poetry included love, patriotism, nature, family and religion. They were called Fireside Poets because poems were read aloud at the fireside for family entertainment.

The Song of Hiawatha – Henry Wadsworth Longfellow

The Song of Hiawatha is an 1855 epic poem, in trochaic tetrameter, by Henry Wadsworth Longfellow (1807-1882), featuring a Native American hero. Longfellow's poem is a work of American Romantic literature, not a representation of Native American oral tradition. As one of the most popular American Poet of the 1800s he experimented with adapting traditional European poetic forms to uniquely American topics, such as "Song of Hiawatha" and "Paul Revere's Ride." He idealized America's early history and democratic ideals. This poem is a long, narrative poem (tells a story) based on the legend of the Ojibway Tribe. Historically, Hiawatha was an Iroquois chief who helped to unite the Iroquois and contains over 20 sections telling of the adventures of Hiawatha.

Should you ask me, whence these stories?
Whence these legends and traditions,
With the odors of the forest
With the dew and damp of meadows,
With the curling smoke of wigwams,
With the rushing of great rivers,
With their frequent repetitions,
And their wild reverberations
As of thunder in the mountains?
I should answer, I should tell you,
"From the forests and the prairies,
From the great lakes of the Northland,
From the land of the Ojibways,
From the land of the Dacotahs,
From the mountains, moors, and fen-lands
Where the heron, the Shuh-shuh-gah,
Feeds among the reeds and rushes.
I repeat them as I heard them
From the lips of Nawadaha,
The musician, the sweet singer."

Should you ask where Nawadaha
Found these songs so wild and wayward,
Found these legends and traditions,
I should answer, I should tell you,
"In the bird's-nests of the forest,
In the lodges of the beaver,
In the hoof-prints of the bison,

In the eyry of the eagle!
"All the wild-fowl sang them to him,
In the moorlands and the fen-lands,
In the melancholy marshes;
Chetowaik, the plover, sang them,
Mahng, the loon, the wild-goose, Wawa,
The blue heron, the Shuh-shuh-gah,
And the grouse, the Mushkodasa!"

If still further you should ask me,
Saying, "Who was Nawadaha?
Tell us of this Nawadaha,"
I should answer your inquiries
Straightway in such words as follow.
"In the vale of Tawasentha,
In the green and silent valley,
By the pleasant water-courses,
Dwelt the singer Nawadaha.
Round about the Indian village
Spread the meadows and the corn-fields,
And beyond them stood the forest,
Stood the groves of singing pine-trees,
Green in Summer, white in Winter,
Ever sighing, ever singing.
"And the pleasant water-courses,
You could trace them through the valley,
By the rushing in the Spring-time,
By the alders in the Summer,
By the white fog in the Autumn,
By the black line in the Winter;
And beside them dwelt the singer,
In the vale of Tawasentha,
In the green and silent valley.
"There he sang of Hiawatha,
Sang the Song of Hiawatha,
Sang his wondrous birth and being,
How he prayed and how he fasted,
How he lived, and toiled, and suffered,
That the tribes of men might prosper,
That he might advance his people!"

Ye who love the haunts of Nature,
Love the sunshine of the meadow,
Love the shadow of the forest,
Love the wind among the branches,
And the rain-shower and the snow-storm,
And the rushing of great rivers
Through their palisades of pine-trees,
And the thunder in the mountains,
Whose innumerable echoes
Flap like eagles in their eyries;--
Listen to these wild traditions,
To this Song of Hiawatha!
Ye who love a nation's legends,

Love the ballads of a people,
That like voices from afar off
Call to us to pause and listen,
Speak in tones so plain and childlike,
Scarcely can the ear distinguish
Whether they are sung or spoken;--
Listen to this Indian Legend,
To this Song of Hiawatha!
Ye whose hearts are fresh and simple,
Who have faith in God and Nature,
Who believe that in all ages
Every human heart is human,
That in even savage bosoms
There are longings, yearnings, strivings
For the good they comprehend not,
That the feeble hands and helpless,
Groping blindly in the darkness,
Touch God's right hand in that darkness
And are lifted up and strengthened;--
Listen to this simple story,
To this Song of Hiawatha!

Ye, who sometimes, in your rambles
Through the green lanes of the country,
Where the tangled barberry-bushes
Hang their tufts of crimson berries
Over stone walls gray with mosses,
Pause by some neglected graveyard,
For a while to muse, and ponder
On a half-effaced inscription,
Written with little skill of song-craft,
Homely phrases, but each letter
Full of hope and yet of heart-break,
Full of all the tender pathos
Of the Here and the Hereafter;--
Stay and read this rude inscription,
Read this Song of Hiawatha!

Old Ironsides -- By Oliver Wendell Holmes Sr.

A sort of biting sarcasm is exactly the tone Dr. Oliver Wendell Holmes (1809-1894) set for his most famous work, 'Old Ironsides', which is a poem written in 1830 to commemorate a frigate named the U.S.S. Constitution, written in alternating tetrameter and trimeter syllabic accents. He was a descendant of first American poet, Anne Bradstreet, and during law school, wrote "Old Ironsides"—which saved USS Constitution from destruction. He wrote poetry for fun and worked as a physician.

Ay, tear her tattered ensign down!
Long has it waved on high,
And many an eye has danced to see
That banner in the sky;
Beneath it rung the battle shout,
And burst the cannon's roar;—
The meteor of the ocean air
Shall sweep the clouds no more!

Her deck, once red with heroes' blood
Where knelt the vanquished foe,
When winds were hurrying o'er the flood
And waves were white below,
No more shall feel the victor's tread,
Or know the conquered knee;—
The harpies of the shore shall pluck
The eagle of the sea!

O, better that her shattered hulk
Should sink beneath the wave;
Her thunders shook the mighty deep,
And there should be her grave;
Nail to the mast her holy flag,
Set every thread-bare sail,
And give her to the god of storms,—
The lightning and the gale!

Journal #9: Hiawatha and Old Ironsides:

Respond to the following questions:
Song of Hiawatha:

1. What is the effect of rhythm in the poem Song of Hiawatha on the reader?
2. What is the effect of repetition on the reader?
3. Why do you think the poet might have used unusual word order?

Old Ironsides:
1. Identify two lines in the poem that show the action in this battle were violent.
2. What is the speaker's overall attitude about the demise of the ship?

Journal #10 Paradox Part 2:

Write Y in the blank of each paradox. Write N in the blank if it is not a paradox.

_____ I know that I know nothing.
_____ He was too tired to go to sleep.
_____ I always lie.
_____ Call me if you find my phone.
_____ She'll be your friend through thick and thin.

Write a T for the paradoxes that can be true. Write an F for those that cannot be true.

_____ You have to spend money to save money.
_____ Deep down inside, he's a very shallow person.
_____ Sometimes you must be cruel to be kind.
_____ No one goes to that movie theater; it's too crowded.
_____ "I can resist anything but temptation." - Oscar Wilde

Explain why each statement below is a paradox.

1. Don't go into the water until you know how to swim.

2. Rule #10: Ignore all rules.
3. If you do not have an Internet connection, go to this website for help.

Assignment #2: Theme/image Essay/Art –Due on last day of class for the Semester

Write on one text. *Plan for only two- three body paragraphs and 4 images* or the equivalent. Use your discretion on this assignment for the student. Choose ONE TOPIC from the set of topics below. Make a comment/position on one of the topics, and use quotes with art to highlight the elements that support your position. Remember you are still trying to convey an idea and position, even if you elect to use the artistic approach. You must have a written text accompanying your visuals

Grading Criteria: Art that is Closely tied to the analysis of the text (use at least four images/drawings or something similar; Theoretical sophistication in presenting the artistry in reference to the text and Literary-historical context in the introduction paragraph and, when appropriate, throughout.

Poe literature: 1. Poe often combined elements of horror, romance, and fantasy in his settings to help create a Gothic atmosphere within his works. **"The Raven"** uses the location of a dreary study at night, while the dark corridor outside the room and the rustling of curtains suggest the presence of supernatural attention upon the chamber. The setting establishes a mood that is receptive to the tensions of horror and terror within the poem. How does Poe incorporate a Gothic setting into his poetry (use at least 2-3 examples)?

Dickinson poetry: 1. Dickinson's Explorations of Poetry. Choose one of Dickinson poems and focus on her self-reflexive focus on the function of poetry or the manner in which poetry is created out of reality.

2. Dickinson's Reflections on Conventionality. Choose one of Dickinson poems and explore how she deconstructs conventional thinking. Show how she keeps the idea open and provides different connections and contexts to an idea or an image.

Whitman poetry: 1. Whitman's poetry of the body. Examine "Song of Myself" for its focus on the material realm of the body as a springboard to his explorations of joy in life and/or of connections with others or with God.

2. Whitman's Inclusive "I." Examine the moments in which Whitman includes others in his concept of the singular personal pronoun. What does this inclusiveness suggest about Whitman's philosophical and political views? How does he carry out this vision on the level of language or structure?

Fireside Poets: 1. Examine either Hiawatha or Old Ironsides – how does the presentation of the image reflect several different meanings, and what is the significance of these meanings? Construct a project that displays the greater significance of the poem.

Transcendentalism: 1. Thoreau identified the difference between loneliness and solitude – what are these differences? How did they impact the America in which Thoreau was writing and how did these ideas reflect his approach to self reliance? What significance could we see in these ideas today?

How to do a Poem Analysis

Print out the poem. Most poems can be found online. If you have a book you're allowed to write in, then write in it. Annotate the poem using the following steps:
- identify the rhyme scheme

- identify the meter and any examples of straying from the meter
- if the poem is difficult, summarize each stanza
- circle important words, ambiguous words, and words you need to look up
- circle examples of figurative language
- write questions
- write down insights.
- Draw conclusions based on the information you gathered while annotating.
- Write the poem analysis. The following steps are for how to write a paragraph analysis:

The topic sentence should state the poem's theme (one that may not be so obvious).
The examples, facts, citations from the poem you're analyzing should support your topic sentence.
Provide analysis explaining how your facts support your topic sentence.

Emily Dickinson – Poetry

Emily Dickinson (1830-1886) is, in a sense, a link between her era and the literary sensitivities of the turn of the century. A radical individualist, she was born and spent her life in Amherst, Massachusetts. She loved nature and found deep inspiration in the birds, animals, plants, and changing seasons of the New England countryside.

Dickinson's terse, frequently imagistic style is even more modern and innovative than Whitman's. She never uses two words when one will do, and combines concrete things with abstract ideas in an almost proverbial, compressed style. Her best poems have no fat; many mock current sentimentality, and some are even heretical. She sometimes shows a terrifying existential awareness. Like Poe, she explores the dark and hidden part of the mind, dramatizing death and the grave. Yet she also celebrated simple objects – a flower, a bee.

Throughout her life, she seldom left her home and visitors were few. The people with whom she did come in contact, however, had an enormous impact on her poetry. Dickinson's poetry was heavily influenced by the Metaphysical poets of seventeenth-century England, as well as her reading of the Book of Revelation and her upbringing in a Puritan New England town. The first volume of her work was published posthumously in 1890 and the last in 1955. She died in Amherst in 1886.

Because I could not stop for Death (479)

Because I could not stop for Death –
He kindly stopped for me –
The Carriage held but just Ourselves –
And Immortality.

We slowly drove – He knew no haste
And I had put away
My labor and my leisure too,
For His Civility –

We passed the School, where Children strove
At Recess – in the Ring –
We passed the Fields of Gazing Grain –
We passed the Setting Sun –

Or rather – He passed us –
The Dews drew quivering and chill –
For only Gossamer, my Gown –
My Tippet – only Tulle –

We paused before a House that seemed
A Swelling of the Ground –
The Roof was scarcely visible –
The Cornice – in the Ground –

Since then – 'tis Centuries – and yet
Feels shorter than the Day
I first surmised the Horses' Heads
Were toward Eternity –

There's a certain Slant of light, (320)

There's a certain Slant of light,
Winter Afternoons –
That oppresses, like the Heft
Of Cathedral Tunes –

Heavenly Hurt, it gives us –
We can find no scar,
But internal difference –
Where the Meanings, are –

None may teach it – Any –
'Tis the seal Despair –
An imperial affliction
Sent us of the Air –

When it comes, the Landscape listens –
Shadows – hold their breath –
When it goes, 'tis like the Distance
On the look of Death –

Journal #11: Dickenson:

Different poems have different rhyme schemes. If every two lines rhyme, it is AABB structure, like we see here from *The Raven*:

> as my Hopes have flown **before**.
> Then the bird said "**Nevermore**"

Or it might have ABAB structure, like we see here in *Old Ironsides:*

> Her deck, once red with heroes' **blood**
> Where knelt the vanquished *foe*,
> When winds were hurrying o'er the **flood**
> And waves were white *below*

If the rhyme scheme changes in the next stanza, it will become CDCD, then EFEF, etc with each stanza. If one stanza repeats the rhyme of a previous one, it reverts back to the original rhyme scheme, so you could have ABAB, CDCD, ABAB. Other rhyme schemes include ABCD, ABCD, and ABAB CDCD EE.

Part 1: Select one of Dickenson's poems. Identify and label the poem's rhyme scheme with the appropriate lettering.

Part 2: Identify Metaphorical and hidden deeper meanings of *Because I could Not Stop for Death*:
1. What is the overall Metaphorical meaning of the poem?
2. What is the deeper allegorical meaning of the following lines?
   a. We passed the school where Children strove   At Recess – in the ring –
   b. We passed the Fields of Grazing Grain
   c. We passed the Setting Sun
   d. Or rather – He passed Us --

Unit 3 Transcendentalism

Transcendentalists believe that the basic truths of the universe transcend the physical world and lie beyond the knowledge that can be obtained from the senses. They feel that every individual has the ability to experience God firsthand in his/her intuition. They value nature and believe in the spiritual unity of all life, stating God, humanity, and nature share a universal soul. They feel that nothing in nature is trivial or insignificant; all is symbolic and important.

They also promoted the belief that every human being is born inherently good. Authors include Ralph Waldo Emerson and Henry David Thoreau.

Genre and Style include Poetry, Short Stories, Novels indented to hold readers' attention through dread of a series of terrible possibilities, feature landscapes of dark forests, extreme vegetation, and concealed ruins with horrific rooms and depressed characters.

Henry David Thoreau:
from Walden: *Where I Lived, and What I Lived For*

Henry David Thoreau (1817-1862)w was an American naturalist, essayist, poet, and philosopher. A leading transcendentalist, he is best known for his book Walden, published in 1854, a reflection upon simple living in natural surroundings, and his essay "Civil Disobedience", an argument for disobedience to an unjust state.

I went to the woods because I wished to live deliberately, to front only the essential facts of life, and see if I could not learn what it had to teach, and not, when I came to die, discover that I had not lived. I did not wish to live what was not life, living is so dear; nor did I wish to practice resignation, unless it was quite necessary. I wanted to live deep and suck out all the marrow of life, to live so sturdily and Spartan-like as to put to rout all that was not life, to cut a broad swath and shave close, to drive life into a corner and reduce it to its lowest terms, and, if it proved to be mean, why then to get the whole and genuine meanness of it, and publish its meanness to the world; or if it were sublime, to know it by experience, and be able to give a true account of it in my next excursion. For most men, it appears to me, are in a strange uncertainty about it, whether it is of the devil or of God, and have somewhat hastily concluded that it is the chief end of man here to "glorify God and enjoy him forever."

Journal # 12

1. What might it mean to live "deliberately"?

_____

2. What might be several of the "essential facts" about life that Thoreau wants to "front" (or confront)?

_____

3. What do you think he means when he says he "did not wish to practice resignation"?

_____

4. What does "suck out all the marrow of life" mean to you?

_____

5. What does it mean to "drive life into a corner and reduce it to its lowest terms"?

_____

6. What might this sentence tell us about Thoreau's religious belief?

_____

Journal #13:

Mock Writing based on Dickenson or Thoreau. Start with the phrase "There's a certain Slant of light, _____" OR "I went to the woods because I wished to live_____" -- fill in the blank. Then finish the paragraph stanza with a description of that fits the word/phrase you selected.

Journal #14: Uncle Tom's Cabin Activity: Read the excerpt and respond to the questions

Uncle Tom's Cabin by Harriet Beecher Stowe, Chapter 3: The Husband and Father

"Well, lately Mas'r has been saying that he was a fool to let me marry off the place; that he hates Mr. Shelby and all his tribe, because they are proud, and hold their heads up above him, and that I've got proud notions from you; and he says he won't let me come here any more, and that I shall take a wife and settle down on his place. At first he only scolded and grumbled these things; but yesterday he told me that I should take Mina for a wife, and settle down in a cabin with her, or he would sell me down river."

"Why—but you were married to me, by the minister, as much as if you'd been a white man!" said Eliza, simply.

"Don't you know a slave can't be married? There is no law in this country for that; I can't hold you for my wife, if he chooses to part us. That's why I wish I'd never seen you,—why I wish I'd never been born; it would have been better for us both,—it would have been better for this poor child if he had never been born. All this may happen to him yet!"

"O, but master is so kind!"

"Yes, but who knows?—he may die—and then he may be sold to nobody knows who. What pleasure is it that he is handsome, and smart, and bright? I tell you, Eliza, that a sword will pierce through your soul for every good and pleasant thing your child is or has; it will make him worth too much for you to keep."

The words smote heavily on Eliza's heart; the vision of the trader came before her eyes, and, as if some one had struck her a deadly blow, she turned pale and gasped for breath. She looked nervously out on the verandah, where the boy, tired of the grave conversation, had retired, and where he was riding triumphantly up and down on Mr. Shelby's walking-stick. She would have spoken to tell her husband her fears, but checked herself.

Q&A: Answer each question below.

1. Why does George say he wishes he had never seen Eliza? _____

_____

2. What does George mean when he says "a sword will pierce through your soul for every good and pleasant thing your

child is or has…"? _____

_____

3. Why does Eliza turn pale and gasp for breath? _____

_____

Oh Captain My Captain – Walt Whitman

Born on Long Island, New York, Walt Whitman (1819-1892) was a part-time carpenter, whose brilliant, pioneering work expressed the country's democratic spirit. Whitman was mostly self-taught, he left school at the age of 11 to go to work. Walter Whitman was an American poet, essayist and journalist. A humanist, he was a part of the transition between transcendentalism and realism, incorporating both views in his works. Whitman is among the most influential poets in the American canon, often called the father of free verse. His *Leaves of Grass* (1855), which he rewrote and revised throughout his life, contains "Song of Myself," the most amazingly original poem ever written by an American.

"O Captain! My Captain!" is an extended metaphor poem written in 1865 by Walt Whitman, about the death of American president Abraham Lincoln. The assassination of Lincoln struck him as a deeply personal loss.

O Captain! my Captain! our fearful trip is done,
The ship has weather'd every rack, the prize we sought is won,
The port is near, the bells I hear, the people all exulting,
While follow eyes the steady keel, the vessel grim and daring;
But O heart! heart! heart!
O the bleeding drops of red,
Where on the deck my Captain lies,
Fallen cold and dead.

O Captain! my Captain! rise up and hear the bells;
Rise up—for you the flag is flung—for you the bugle trills,
For you bouquets and ribbon'd wreaths—for you the shores a-crowding,
For you they call, the swaying mass, their eager faces turning;
Here Captain! dear father!
This arm beneath your head!
It is some dream that on the deck,
You've fallen cold and dead.

My Captain does not answer, his lips are pale and still,
My father does not feel my arm, he has no pulse nor will,
The ship is anchor'd safe and sound, its voyage closed and done,
From fearful trip the victor ship comes in with object won;
Exult O shores, and ring O bells!
But I with mournful tread,
Walk the deck my Captain lies,
Fallen cold and dead.

Song of myself – From *Leaves of Grass*:

1

I celebrate myself, and sing myself,
And what I assume you shall assume,
For every atom belonging to me as good belongs to you.

I loafe and invite my soul,
I lean and loafe at my ease observing a spear of summer grass.

My tongue, every atom of my blood, form'd from this soil, this air,
Born here of parents born here from parents the same, and their parents the same,
I, now thirty-seven years old in perfect health begin,
Hoping to cease not till death.

Creeds and schools in abeyance,
Retiring back a while sufficed at what they are, but never forgotten,
I harbor for good or bad, I permit to speak at every hazard,
Nature without check with original energy.

51

The past and present wilt—I have fill'd them, emptied them,
And proceed to fill my next fold of the future.

Listener up there! what have you to confide to me?
Look in my face while I snuff the sidle of evening,
(Talk honestly, no one else hears you, and I stay only a minute longer.)

Do I contradict myself?
Very well then I contradict myself,
(I am large, I contain multitudes.)

I concentrate toward them that are nigh, I wait on the door-slab.

Who has done his day's work? who will soonest be through with his supper?
Who wishes to walk with me?

Will you speak before I am gone? will you prove already too late?

52
The spotted hawk swoops by and accuses me, he complains of my gab and my loitering.

I too am not a bit tamed, I too am untranslatable,
I sound my barbaric yawp over the roofs of the world.

The last scud of day holds back for me,
It flings my likeness after the rest and true as any on the shadow'd wilds,
It coaxes me to the vapor and the dusk.

I depart as air, I shake my white locks at the runaway sun,
I effuse my flesh in eddies, and drift it in lacy jags.
If you want me again look for me under your boot-soles.

You will hardly know who I am or what I mean,
But I shall be good health to you nevertheless,
And filter and fibre your blood.

Failing to fetch me at first keep encouraged,
Missing me one place search another,
I stop somewhere waiting for you.

Journal #15 Whitman:

1. Identify Rhetorical Elements in "O Captain, My Captain!" – use the Devices worksheet to help you.
    Answer the following questions about "O Captain, My Captain!"
    a. "O Captain! My Captain!" was written just after the end of the Civil War. The speaker's description of a captain who dies most likely refers to who? *Abraham Lincoln*
    b. The use of the phrase "my Captain" in the title and throughout the poem suggests that the speaker is what? *Loyal to the captain.*
    c. Which phrase suggests that the ship has survived a difficult situation? *Our fearful Trip*
    d. What does the ship in the poem symbolize? *The United States*
    e. The tone in the third stanza of "O Captian! My Captain" is best described as what? *Mournful*

  f. In line 21 the speaker says, "the ship is anchor'd safe and sound." The idea of safety is ironic, or unexpected because . . . ? *The captain is dead on the deck,*

  g.

2. What does Whitman mean when he says, "If you want me again, look for me under your boot-soles"?
  1. His poetry is everywhere.
  2. He is a "grass-roots" poet.
  3. He is a common man, just like anyone else.
  4. *all of the above*
  5. none of the above

In Song of Myself excerpt,

3. Walt Whitman expresses his identification with
  1. death
  2. *nature*
  3. his mother
  4. time
  5. none of the above

4. Who does the narrator celebrate and sing?
5. What is an example of imagery? An example of a figure of speech?

Assignment #3 - Huck Finn:

Write on one text. *Plan for only two – three body paragraphs.* Choose ONE topic from the set of topics below. Each body paragraph will require a minimum of two quotations from the text properly embedded and properly cited according to MLA citation. Construct a logical line of argument from thesis to topic sentences and use close analysis of text to prove your argument.

The writing process—drafting, re-drafting and editing—**1) the thesis and topic sentences.** Review this with me before working on rough first draft – use a scratch outline/notes to generate these. Then, work on a **2) first draft** of two pages minimum. If you haven't shown it to me by the Friday before the second draft is due, and then; **3) second draft** (at least three pages).

Grading Criteria

- Substantive points of argument for thesis and topic sentences; and
- Close/detailed/precise analysis of the text (use at least three quotations per body paragraph and analyze them closely).
- Theoretical sophistication
- Literary-historical context in the introduction paragraph and, when appropriate, throughout.

As you choose one of the topics below, be sure to frame your argument based on that topic as it can be shown as a commentary on the nature of American literature in general. Thus you'll be formulating a theory of American literature from the basis of your close analysis of that text.

Twain, *The Adventures of Huckleberry Finn*

1. The problem of the ending: Critics have long puzzled over the last chapters of *The Adventures of Huckleberry Finn*, not only for the games Tom and Huck play with Jim but also for Huck's own departure and his unsatisfying parting with Jim. In these chapters, Jim seems to return to the Uncle Tom caricature, and Twain even adds another stereotype, the Sambo, in Nat. After all the progress in their friendship, this is a disheartening return to the demeaning subordination of Jim to the European-American characters. Why does Twain close down the building friendship between Huck and Jim as Huck aligns himself with Tom? What could this shift signify about the prospects of European Americans freeing themselves from their racial conditioning in the years following the Civil War?

2. Huck's moral quandary: At the center of the novel, Twain places Huck's moral quandary between slaveholding morality and egalitarian morality. He regards the slaveholding morality to be normative and even natural, even though he's a social outsider himself. Trace Huck's path as he wrestles with the process of overcoming his racial conditioning by virtue of his intimate friendship with Jim. Does Huck arrive fully at a new vision, fully jettisoning his former conditioning, or does he end without resolving the quandary? What Biblical implication does Huck unknowingly advocate in his friendship with Jim? Keep your focus on Twain's process of shaping these moments for Huck and his rhetorical relationship to his post-Civil War readers.

3. The river as nature—realism *versus* romanticism: Twain's own time on the Mississippi as a riverboat captain gave him vivid memories for the construction of his novel. The Mississippi, in this novel, comes to represent a space apart from society, a natural place untainted by human corruption. Even so, human corruption is constantly encroaching on the raft, forcing Huck to grapple with difficult social conflicts. Twain seems to move back and forth between romanticizing the river as a beneficial of moral influence on Huck and showing the inability to maintain a utopia in the world. What function does the romanticization of the river serve in the novel? Why does Twain continually interrupt that romanticized river with the realism of social problems? What does this binary say about American thought in general?

4. Social law or norm *versus* conscience: Huck's central struggle is between what his racist society tells him about his proper relationship with Jim and what his heart tells him about it. Twain shows that that simple binary is made more complex as he explores Huck's "deformed conscience," the idea that racial conditioning has corrupted even his private conscience. Write an essay analyzing the interplay of these binary terms--the social norm *versus* the individual conscience. Does the novel resolve this dialectic or does it leave it unresolved, thus commenting on the intransigence of the norm? From where does the conscience get its vision? What biblical construct can we asses from this conflict ?

5. Idea of Huck as every American: *The Adventures of Huckleberry Finn* is often regarded by critics as the paradigmatic American novel and its hero, Huck Finn, comes to stand in for the ideal of the American--independent-minded, ingenious, connected to nature, and perspicacious. If Huck is to represent the American, that category becomes confined within a particular gender and ethnic status: the true American as the white boy. Write an essay analyzing Huck's American characteristics. Come up with key character traits in Huck that can be seen as a figurative representation of American traits. Be sure to show the problematic nature of this idea due to its gender and ethnic scriptedness. If Huck has an ambiguous moral nature, does Twain suggest the same of America?

6. Persistence of domesticity or Domesticity *versus* naturalness: Huck tries to escape domesticity from the beginning of the novel when he is unhappy with the Widow Douglas's "pecking." Even so, Huck is constantly finding himself in domestic scenes--the Grangerfords, the Wilks, Aunt Sally's house, and even the domesticated raft. Write an essay that examines the binary between domesticity and naturalness, showing how the binary functions and how it also breaks down. What are the characteristics of domestication for Huck and what are the characteristics of the natural life? Is the natural life an ideal which can be attained or is it merely a momentary indulgence or escape from domesticity?

Journal #16 Paradox part 3:

Remember, a ***paradox*** is a contradictory statement, situation or idea. Below are quotations from literature. Explain why each is a paradox.

1) Robert Frost, "The Tuft of Flowers"
"Men work together," I told him from the heart,
"Whether they work together or apart."

2) Oscar Wilde, "Lady Windemere's Fan"
I can resist everything except temptation.

3) Emily Dickinson, "Poems, Series 2
I'm nobody! Who are you?
Are you nobody, too?

Unit 4 Realism 1860-1914

Realism was a reaction against Romanticism and Neoclassicism of the earlier years. At this time, facts were seen as more important than the intellectualism or the emotional. Realism treats nature objectively, but views it as orderly, tells the stories of everyday people, and involves the use of details that are more important than plot. In diction, Realism seeks to use natural language, the language of "everyman."

The genre and style of this movement include novels and short stories, an objective narrator, does not tell reader how to interpret story and includes dialogue includes voices from around the country. Realism also involved social realism, with aims to change a specific social problem, and aesthetic realism, which is art that insists on detailing the world exactly as one sees it.

Walt Whitman is a bridge between ***Romanticism/Transcendentalism and Realism***. Mark Twain is one of the main authors of this period, known to be the ***"father of the American novel"*** from his book *The Adventures of Huckleberry Finn*, which many claim is the first modern novel, and is often considered the Great American Novel. Writings of Ambrose Bierce, Stephen Crane, and *The Narrative of the Life of Frederick Douglass,* are also works of Realism. Regional works include The Awakening. Ethan Frome, and *My Antonia* (some say modern). Other authors include Willa Cather and Kate Chopin.

Samuel Clemens, also known by his pen name of ***Mark Twain,*** grew up in the Mississippi River frontier town of Hannibal, Missouri. Ernest Hemingway's well-known statement, that all of American literature comes from one great book: Twain's *Adventures of Huckleberry Finn;* shows Twain's high place in the tradition. Twain's style, based on strong, realistic, everyday American speech, gave American writers a new appreciation for their national voice. Twain was the first major author to come from the heart of the country, and he captured its distinctive and humorous slang and iconoclasm.

Chief Joseph – "I will Fight no more forever"

Chief Joseph of the Nez Perce (1840?-1904) was known to his people as "Thunder Traveling to the Loftier Mountain Heights." He led his people in an attempt to resist the takeover of their lands in the Oregon Territory by white settlers. In 1877, the Nez Perce were ordered to move to a reservation in Idaho. Chief Joseph agreed at first. But after members of his tribe killed a group of settlers, he tried to flee to Canada with his followers, traveling over 1500 miles through Oregon, Washington, Idaho, and Montana. Along the way they fought several battles with the pursuing U.S. Army. Chief Joseph spoke these words when they finally surrendered on October 5th, 1877.

Chief Joseph - Thunder Traveling to the Loftier Mountain Heights – 1877

Tell General Howard I know his heart. What he told me before, I have it in my heart. I am tired of fighting. Our Chiefs are killed; Looking Glass is dead, Ta Hool Hool Shute is dead. The old men are all dead. It is the young men who say yes or no. He who led on the young men is dead. It is cold, and we have no blankets; the little children are freezing to death. My people, some of them, have run away to the hills, and have no blankets, no food. No one knows where they are - perhaps freezing to death. I want to have time to look for my children, and see how many of them I can find. Maybe I shall find them among the dead. Hear me, my Chiefs! I am tired; my heart is sick and sad. From where the sun now stands I will fight no more forever.

Journal #17:

Realism diary entries – from the point of view of either Huck Finn or Chief Joseph, write 2-3 diary entries that shows the realism of the time, setting, and events.

Man With the Hoe -- By Edwin Markham

This poem, which was written after seeing Millet's world-famous painting, was published in 1899 by a California school-principal, and made a profound impression. It has been hailed as "the battle-cry of the next thousand years"

BOWED by the weight of centuries he leans
Upon his hoe and gazes on the ground,
The emptiness of ages in his face,
And on his back the burden of the world.
Who made him dead to rapture and despair,   *5*
A thing that grieves not and that never hopes,
Stolid and stunned, a brother to the ox?
Who loosened and let down this brutal jaw?
Whose was the hand that slanted back this brow?
Whose breath blew out the light within this brain?   *10*

Is this the thing the Lord God made and gave
To have dominion over sea and land;
To trace the stars and search the heavens for power;
To feel the passion of Eternity?
Is this the dream He dreamed who shaped the suns   *15*
And marked their ways upon the ancient deep?
Down all the stretch of Hell to its last gulf
There is no shape more terrible than this—
More tongued with censure of the world's blind greed—
More filled with signs and portents for the soul—   *20*
More fraught with menace to the universe.

What gulfs between him and the seraphim!
Slave of the wheel of labor, what to him
Are Plato and the swing of Pleiades?
What the long reaches of the peaks of song,   *25*
The rift of dawn, the reddening of the rose?
Through this dread shape the suffering ages look;
Time's tragedy is in that aching stoop;
Through this dread shape humanity betrayed,
Plundered, profaned and disinherited,   *30*
Cries protest to the Judges of the World,
A protest that is also prophecy.

O masters, lords and rulers in all lands,
Is this the handiwork you give to God,
This monstrous thing distorted and soul-quenched?   *35*
How will you ever straighten up this shape;
Touch it again with immortality;
Give back the upward looking and the light;
Rebuild in it the music and the dream;
Make right the immemorial infamies,   *40*
Perfidious wrongs, immedicable woes?

O masters, lords and rulers in all lands,
How will the Future reckon with this Man?
How answer his brute question in that hour
When whirlwinds of rebellion shake the world?   *45*
How will it be with kingdoms and with kings—
With those who shaped him to the thing he is—
When this dumb Terror shall reply to God,

After the silence of the centuries?

Read The Last Leaf from your reading list then answer these questions:

<u>**Journal #18: The Last Leaf Comprehension Questions**</u>

1.   How is pneumonia described in the story?

2.   What does the doctor mean by "lining up on the side of the undertaker?"

3.   What comparisons describe Johnsy's appearance and feelings?

4.   Describe Mr. Behrman's relationship with Sue and Johnsy.

5.   Why does Sue call the leaf that Mr. Behrman painted his "masterpiece?"

6.   What was the twist in the story?

7.   Literary devices – There are examples of verbal and dramatic irony in the story. What events from the story are examples of verbal irony? Why is it important? What is an example of dramatic irony? Why is that important?

<u>**T.S. Eliot (1888–1965). Prufrock and Other Observations. 1920.**</u>

1. The Love Song of J. Alfred Prufrock

*S'io credesse che mia risposta fosse
A persona che mai tornasse al mondo,
Questa fiamma staria senza piu scosse.
Ma perciocche giammai di questo fondo
Non torno vivo alcun, s'i'odo il vero,
Senza tema d'infamia ti rispondo.*

LET us go then, you and I,
When the evening is spread out against the sky
Like a patient etherized upon a table;
Let us go, through certain half-deserted streets,
The muttering retreats
Of restless nights in one-night cheap hotels
And sawdust restaurants with oyster-shells:
Streets that follow like a tedious argument
Of insidious intent
To lead you to an overwhelming question….
Oh, do not ask, "What is it?"
Let us go and make our visit.

In the room the women come and go

Talking of Michelangelo.

The yellow fog that rubs its back upon the window-panes,
The yellow smoke that rubs its muzzle on the window-panes
Licked its tongue into the corners of the evening,
Lingered upon the pools that stand in drains,
Let fall upon its back the soot that falls from chimneys,
Slipped by the terrace, made a sudden leap,
And seeing that it was a soft October night,
Curled once about the house, and fell asleep.

And indeed there will be time
For the yellow smoke that slides along the street,
Rubbing its back upon the window panes;
There will be time, there will be time
To prepare a face to meet the faces that you meet;
There will be time to murder and create,
And time for all the works and days of hands
That lift and drop a question on your plate;
Time for you and time for me,
And time yet for a hundred indecisions,
And for a hundred visions and revisions,
Before the taking of a toast and tea.

In the room the women come and go
Talking of Michelangelo.

And indeed there will be time
To wonder, "Do I dare?" and, "Do I dare?"
Time to turn back and descend the stair,
With a bald spot in the middle of my hair—
(They will say: "How his hair is growing thin!")
My morning coat, my collar mounting firmly to the chin,
My necktie rich and modest, but asserted by a simple pin—
(They will say: "But how his arms and legs are thin!")
Do I dare
Disturb the universe?
In a minute there is time
For decisions and revisions which a minute will reverse.

For I have known them all already, known them all:
Have known the evenings, mornings, afternoons,
I have measured out my life with coffee spoons;
I know the voices dying with a dying fall

Beneath the music from a farther room.
  So how should I presume?

And I have known the eyes already, known them all—
The eyes that fix you in a formulated phrase,
And when I am formulated, sprawling on a pin,
When I am pinned and wriggling on the wall,
Then how should I begin
To spit out all the butt-ends of my days and ways?
  And how should I presume?

And I have known the arms already, known them all—

Arms that are braceleted and white and bare
(But in the lamplight, downed with light brown hair!)
Is it perfume from a dress
That makes me so digress?
Arms that lie along a table, or wrap about a shawl.
  And should I then presume?
  And how should I begin?

. . . .

Shall I say, I have gone at dusk through narrow streets
And watched the smoke that rises from the pipes
Of lonely men in shirt-sleeves, leaning out of windows?…

I should have been a pair of ragged claws
Scuttling across the floors of silent seas.

. . . .

And the afternoon, the evening, sleeps so peacefully!
Smoothed by long fingers,
Asleep … tired … or it malingers,
Stretched on the floor, here beside you and me.
Should I, after tea and cakes and ices,
Have the strength to force the moment to its crisis?
But though I have wept and fasted, wept and prayed,
Though I have seen my head (grown slightly bald) brought in upon a platter,
I am no prophet—and here's no great matter;
I have seen the moment of my greatness flicker,
And I have seen the eternal Footman hold my coat, and snicker,
And in short, I was afraid.

And would it have been worth it, after all,
After the cups, the marmalade, the tea,
Among the porcelain, among some talk of you and me,
Would it have been worth while,
To have bitten off the matter with a smile,
To have squeezed the universe into a ball
To roll it toward some overwhelming question,
To say: "I am Lazarus, come from the dead,
Come back to tell you all, I shall tell you all"—
If one, settling a pillow by her head,
  Should say: "That is not what I meant at all;
  That is not it, at all."

And would it have been worth it, after all,
Would it have been worth while,
After the sunsets and the dooryards and the sprinkled streets,
After the novels, after the teacups, after the skirts that trail along the floor—
And this, and so much more?—
It is impossible to say just what I mean!
But as if a magic lantern threw the nerves in patterns on a screen:
Would it have been worth while
If one, settling a pillow or throwing off a shawl,
And turning toward the window, should say:
  "That is not it at all,
  That is not what I meant, at all."

. . . .

No! I am not Prince Hamlet, nor was meant to be;
Am an attendant lord, one that will do
To swell a progress, start a scene or two,

Advise the prince; no doubt, an easy tool,
Deferential, glad to be of use,
Politic, cautious, and meticulous;
Full of high sentence, but a bit obtuse;
At times, indeed, almost ridiculous—
Almost, at times, the Fool.

I grow old … I grow old …
I shall wear the bottoms of my trousers rolled.

Shall I part my hair behind? Do I dare to eat a peach?
I shall wear white flannel trousers, and walk upon the beach.
I have heard the mermaids singing, each to each.

I do not think that they will sing to me.

I have seen them riding seaward on the waves
Combing the white hair of the waves blown back
When the wind blows the water white and black.

We have lingered in the chambers of the sea
By sea-girls wreathed with seaweed red and brown
Til human voices wake us, and we drown.

Journal #19: Prufrock Complete this chart:

"The Love Song of J. Alfred Prufrock": Lines for Close Analysis	Guiding Questions
1) Lines 1-12	1) Who is the speaker of the poem and to whom is the poem addressed?
2) Lines 1-14	2) Where is the speaker? Describe the time of day, place, etc. What parts of the poem support your answer?
3) Lines 1-14	3) Identify two SIMILES in the opening stanza. What do these similes suggest about what is being compared to something else?
4) Lines 13-14	4) What room is the speaker describing?
5) Lines 15-22	5) Identify the primary METAPHOR in this stanza. In other words, to what does the poet indirectly liken the yellow fog? Note specific elements/words from the poem to support your answer.
6) Lines 23-34	6) What is the primary argument of this stanza? Sum up the argument in one sentence.

7) Lines 37-48	7) What is the speaker's emotional state at this point in the poem? What are his primary concerns?
8) Line 51	8) What does the speaker mean in line 51?
9) Lines 49-69	9) Identify the poem's use of REPETITION? What effect does repetition have on the poem's meaning?
10) Lines 49-69	10) What is the speaker's TONE at this point in the poem? Support with text.
11) Line 66	11) Re-read line 66. What stands out about the act of digressing?
13) Lines 75-86	13) Do you think the speaker himself is digressing? Identify parts of the poem to support your answer.
14) Lines 90-98	14) Describe the speaker's relationship to speaking itself? Is he effective at expressing himself and/or telling a story? Why or why not?
15) Lines 120-125	15) Has the speaker finally admitted his primary concern? What effect does "growing old" have on the speaker's socializing?
16) Lines 129-131	16) What is the speaker's final tone? Explain.

Modernism and Post Modernism

Modernism is a period in literary history which started around the early 1900s and continued until the early 1940s. Modernist writers in general rebelled against clear-cut storytelling and formulaic verse from the 19th century. Instead, many of them told fragmented stories which reflected the fragmented state of society during and after World War I.

Many Modernists wrote in free verse and they included many countries and cultures in their poems. Some wrote using numerous points-of-view or even used a "stream-of-consciousness" style. These writing styles further demonstrate the way the scattered state of society affected the work of writers at that time. The Modernist ideas of Imagism and the work of William Carlos Williams, for example, continue to have a great influence on writers today.

By the 1950s, a new generation of Postmodern poets came to the forefront. Adding "post" in front of the word "Modern" showed that this new period was different than the one before it, yet was influenced by it.

Postmodern literature is a literary movement that eschews absolute meaning and instead emphasizes play, fragmentation, metafiction, and intertextuality. The literary movement rose to prominence in the late 1950s and early 1960s as a reaction to modernist literature's quest for meaning in light of the significant human rights violations of World War II.

Final Assignment #4:   Modern/ Postmodern Response paper

For this assignment *Plan for only three paragraphs*. Choose ONE TOPIC from the set of topics below. Each body paragraph will require a minimum of two quotations from the text properly embedded and properly cited according to MLA citation. This Assignment is a personal response to the ideas, themes, or emotions presented, how you think they reflect the Modern or Post Modern aspect, and how you would evaluate the text in the context of Christianity and/or your life.

Gilman, "The Yellow Wall-paper" AND "Jury of her peers" Gladspell

1. Madness as a liberation. Most metaphors of madness treat it as a sort of descent into incapacity, almost a descent into the loss of one's very humanity. Gilman represents the real world as it's lived by women in the nineteenth century under the seemingly benign totalitarianism of patriarchy as a sort of nightmare. In this physical world of confinement, endorsed initially by the narrator's own mental confinement, Gilman opens the space of liberation exactly where one doesn't expect it--in the realm of madness. Write an essay analyzing Gilman's use of madness as a space of liberation rather than as a space of confinement or debility.

2. Release from identification with the Oppressor. In any system of oppression, the oppressed person is conditioned to identify with the oppressor. Instead of identifying their own interests as separate and even opposed to those of the oppressor, the oppressed person is conditioned with years of training in all forms of culture to see her or his interests as one with or submerged under the interests of the oppressor. At some point, for some reason, the oppressed person can wake up to her oppression and see that she has been identifying with the person or the system that has been limiting her freedom. Pick either the Gilman story or the Gladspell story and write an essay tracing the unnamed narrator's shift from identifying with her oppressor to regarding him as a threat to her freedom.

3. Compare and contrast "A Jury of Her Peers" by Susan Glaspell and "The Yellow Wallpaper" by Charlotte Perkins. How do the two characters have the same mental illness/subject to the same oppression? OR – how does each text showcase the start of the genre of feminist literature in America?

Hemingway "old man and the sea" : 1. What is it to be defeated? "A man can be destroyed but not defeated," says the old man after the first shark attack. At the end of the story, is the old man defeated? Why or why not?

2. The significance of minor characters: *The Old Man and the Sea* is, essentially, the story of a single character. Indeed, other than the old man, only one human being receives any kind of prolonged attention. Discuss the role of Manolin in the novella. Is he necessary to the book?

3. Religious Symbolism: Discuss religious symbolism in *The Old Man and the Sea*. To what effect does Hemingway employ such images? What does this symbolism mean for the text as a whole?

Poets

Langston Hughes: What is Hughes's over-arching view on America? However, Hughes believed that African Americans deserved equality and presented a vision of America as a racially equal country. He accepted that the path would not be easy, but emphasized that the struggle for equality was worth enduring. How does he show this in his poetry?

T.S. Eliot: How does Eliot use the relationships between men and women to comment on society and culture? Why is "Prufrock" a "love song"? The poem ends with Prufrock drowning with his love in the ocean. Is this ending real or some kind of dream? What elements from the poem show this? How does it relate to the rest of the poem?

Robert Frost: 1. Do you think the speaker regrets his choice, or is happy about it? Why? Why does the choice of roads in "The Road Not Taken" make so much difference to the speaker years later? What might the two roads represent?

2. In "Stopping by the woods on a snowy evening" what is the effect of Frost's use of repetition in the final two lines? A temporary escape from reality is revealed in "Stopping by Woods on a Snowy Evening." Why do you think that people at times need to find this type of temporary escape? Do you view the ending in a positive or a negative light? Why? What might the woods and snow and dark symbolize?

Maya Angelou: 1. What, in your opinion, does the caged bird symbolize? What role does the free bird play in "Caged Bird"? How do we know the caged bird is a symbolic bird?" Use evidence from the poem to support your answer.

   3.   "Still I Rise" is a poem about African American triumph over white oppression. How does Angelou's choice of imagery, simile, and metaphor, create a message of affirmation that is powerful yet not frightening? Who is "you" in "Still I Rise"? How do we know?

William Carlos Williams
On September 17, 1883, William Carlos Williams was born in Rutherford, New Jersey. He received his MD from the University of Pennsylvania, where he met and befriended Ezra Pound (a famous British Poet). Pound became a great influence on his writing, and in 1913 arranged for the London publication of Williams's second collection, The Tempers. He was one of the principal poets of the Imagist movement (describes images with simple language and great focus). Williams sought to invent an entirely fresh—and singularly American—poetic, whose subject matter was centered on the everyday circumstances of life and the lives of common people. He continued writing up until his death in New Jersey on March 4, 1963.

The Red Wheelbarrow   so much depends
                                                                                      upon

a red wheel
barrow

glazed with rain
water

beside the white
chickens.

The Great Figure

Among the rain
and lights
I saw the figure 5
in gold
on a red
firetruck
moving
tense
unheeded
to gong clangs
siren howls
and wheels rumbling
through the dark city.

This Is Just To Say

I have eaten
the plums
that were in
the icebox

and which
you were probably
saving
for breakfast

Forgive me
they were delicious
so sweet
and so cold

Journal #20 Modern poetry:

Rewrite one of the Williams poems above onto a sheet of notebook paper or type it and print it out. You can also find another Williams poem for this activity if you wish, but it is not required. Try to use larger text.

Using highlighters or colored pens/pencils. Select one color for alliteration, one for assonance, one for imagery, and one for repetition/ onomatopoeia. Once you have completed this, draw a picture that reflects the image idea presented in your selected.

Robert Frost

Robert Lee Frost (March 26, 1874 – January 29, 1963) was an American poet. His work was initially published in England before it was published in America. He is highly regarded for his realistic depictions of rural life and his command of American colloquial speech.[5] His work frequently employed settings from rural life in New England in the early twentieth century, using them to examine complex social and philosophical themes. One of the most popular and critically respected American poets of the twentieth century,[6] Frost was honored frequently during his lifetime, receiving four Pulitzer Prizes for Poetry.

The Road Not Taken

Two roads diverged in a yellow wood,
And sorry I could not travel both
And be one traveler, long I stood
And looked down one as far as I could
To where it bent in the undergrowth;

Then took the other, as just as fair,
And having perhaps the better claim,
Because it was grassy and wanted wear;
Though as for that the passing there
Had worn them really about the same,

And both that morning equally lay
In leaves no step had trodden black.
Oh, I kept the first for another day!
Yet knowing how way leads on to way,
I doubted if I should ever come back.

I shall be telling this with a sigh
Somewhere ages and ages hence:
Two roads diverged in a wood, and I—
I took the one less traveled by,
And that has made all the difference.

Mending Wall

Something there is that doesn't love a wall,
That sends the frozen-ground-swell under it,
And spills the upper boulders in the sun,
And makes gaps even two can pass abreast.
The work of hunters is another thing:
I have come after them and made repair
Where they have left not one stone on a stone,
But they would have the rabbit out of hiding,
To please the yelping dogs. The gaps I mean,
No one has seen them made or heard them made,
But at spring mending-time we find them there.
I let my neighbor know beyond the hill;
And on a day we meet to walk the line
And set the wall between us once again.
We keep the wall between us as we go.
To each the boulders that have fallen to each.
And some are loaves and some so nearly balls
We have to use a spell to make them balance:
'Stay where you are until our backs are turned!'
We wear our fingers rough with handling them.
Oh, just another kind of out-door game,
One on a side. It comes to little more:
There where it is we do not need the wall:
He is all pine and I am apple orchard.
My apple trees will never get across
And eat the cones under his pines, I tell him.
He only says, 'Good fences make good neighbors'.
Spring is the mischief in me, and I wonder
If I could put a notion in his head:
'Why do they make good neighbors? Isn't it
Where there are cows?
But here there are no cows.
Before I built a wall I'd ask to know
What I was walling in or walling out,
And to whom I was like to give offence.
Something there is that doesn't love a wall,
That wants it down.' I could say 'Elves' to him,
But it's not elves exactly, and I'd rather
He said it for himself. I see him there
Bringing a stone grasped firmly by the top
In each hand, like an old-stone savage armed.
He moves in darkness as it seems to me~
Not of woods only and the shade of trees.
He will not go behind his father's saying,
And he likes having thought of it so well
He says again, "Good fences make good neighbors."

<u>Journal #21: Frost</u>
<u>**Answer the follow questions about the above poems**</u>

1. What is the rhyme scheme? – mark it on the poems.
2. What decision does the speaker have to make in *The Road not Taken*?

3. Infer the season in both poems. How do you know?

4. Explain why the reader doubts he'll ever come back to travel the first road in *the Road Not Taken*.

5. Describe the conflict the speaker feels in both *The Road not Taken* and *The Mending Wall*.

Langston Hughes

Langston Hughes was first recognized as an important literary figure during the 1920s, a period known as the "Harlem Renaissance" because of the number of emerging black writers and artists. First published in 1921 in The Crisis — official magazine of the National Association for the Advancement of Colored People (NAACP) — "The Negro Speaks of Rivers", which became Hughes's signature poem, was collected in his first book of poetry The Weary Blues (1926).

The Negro Speaks of Rivers

I've known rivers:
I've known rivers ancient as the world and older than the
flow of human blood in human veins.
My soul has grown deep like the rivers.

I bathed in the Euphrates when dawns were young.
I built my hut near the Congo and it lulled me to sleep.
I looked upon the Nile and raised the pyramids above it.
I heard the singing of the Mississippi when Abe Lincoln
went down to New Orleans, and I've seen its muddy
bosom turn all golden in the sunset.

I've known rivers:
Ancient, dusky rivers.
My soul has grown deep like the rivers.

The Weary Blues

Droning a drowsy syncopated tune,
Rocking back and forth to a mellow croon,
I heard a Negro play.
Down on Lenox Avenue the other night
By the pale dull pallor of an old gas light
He did a lazy sway . . .
He did a lazy sway . . .

To the tune o' those Weary Blues.
With his ebony hands on each ivory key
He made that poor piano moan with melody.
O Blues!
Swaying to and fro on his rickety stool
He played that sad raggy tune like a musical fool.
Sweet Blues!
Coming from a black man's soul.
O Blues!
In a deep song voice with a melancholy tone
I heard that Negro sing, that old piano moan—
"Ain't got nobody in all this world,
Ain't got nobody but ma self.
I's gwine to quit ma frownin'
And put ma troubles on the shelf."

Thump, thump, thump, went his foot on the floor.
He played a few chords then he sang some more—
"I got the Weary Blues
And I can't be satisfied.
Got the Weary Blues
And can't be satisfied—
I ain't happy no mo'
And I wish that I had died."
And far into the night he crooned that tune.
The stars went out and so did the moon.
The singer stopped playing and went to bed
While the Weary Blues echoed through his head.
He slept like a rock or a man that's dead.

Journal #22: Hughes/Harlem Renaissance

Have the student do brief research on the Harlem Renaissance, what it was, and who some of the artists and writers of that movement were.

Erasure, or blackout poetry, is a way of showcasing themes and ideas from a poem in a creative way. For this project, the student will select one poem by Langston (either one from above or another poem they select by Langston). They will copy it out or print it out. Then they will put a box around the words they wish to keep. These words can create a sentence about the theme or create a new poem on that theme.

After the student has selected the words from the poem they wish to focus on, they will take a black marker and draw thick lines over the rest until only the selected words remain visible. Then the student must write or present how their new poem or writing showcases an aspect of the Harlem Renaissance and reflects the theme of the poem.

Maya Angelou

Maya Angelou (April 4, 1928 – May 28, 2014) was an American poet, memoirist, and civil rights activist. She published seven autobiographies, three books of essays, several books of poetry, and was credited with a list of plays, movies, and television shows spanning over 50 years. She received dozens of awards and more than 50 honorary degrees. Angelou is best known for her series of seven autobiographies, which focus on her childhood and early adult experiences. The first, *I Know Why the Caged Bird Sings* (1969), tells of her life up to the age of 17 and brought her international recognition and acclaim.

Still I Rise
You may write me down in history
With your bitter, twisted lies,
You may trod me in the very dirt

But still, like dust, I'll rise.

Does my sassiness upset you?
Why are you beset with gloom?

'Cause I walk like I've got oil wells
Pumping in my living room.

Just like moons and like suns,
With the certainty of tides,
Just like hopes springing high,
Still I'll rise.

Did you want to see me broken?
Bowed head and lowered eyes?
Shoulders falling down like teardrops,
Weakened by my soulful cries?

Does my haughtiness offend you?
Don't you take it awful hard
'Cause I laugh like I've got gold mines
Diggin' in my own backyard.

You may shoot me with your words,
You may cut me with your eyes,
You may kill me with your hatefulness,
But still, like air, I'll rise.

Does my sexiness upset you?
Does it come as a surprise
That I dance like I've got diamonds
At the meeting of my thighs?

Out of the huts of history's shame
I rise
Up from a past that's rooted in pain
I rise
I'm a black ocean, leaping and wide,
Welling and swelling I bear in the tide.

Leaving behind nights of terror and fear
I rise
Into a daybreak that's wondrously clear
I rise
Bringing the gifts that my ancestors gave,
I am the dream and the hope of the slave.
I rise
I rise
I rise.

Caged Bird

A free bird leaps
on the back of the wind
and floats downstream
till the current ends
and dips his wing
in the orange sun rays
and dares to claim the sky.

But a bird that stalks
down his narrow cage
can seldom see through
his bars of rage
his wings are clipped and
his feet are tied
so he opens his throat to sing.

The caged bird sings
with a fearful trill
of things unknown
but longed for still
and his tune is heard
on the distant hill
for the caged bird
sings of freedom.

The free bird thinks of another breeze
and the trade winds soft through the sighing trees
and the fat worms waiting on a dawn bright lawn
and he names the sky his own

But a caged bird stands on the grave of dreams
his shadow shouts on a nightmare scream
his wings are clipped and his feet are tied
so he opens his throat to sing.

The caged bird sings
with a fearful trill
of things unknown
but longed for still
and his tune is heard
on the distant hill
for the caged bird
sings of freedom.

Journal #23: Angelou
Identify and explain the following elements of one of the above poems in your own words:
Title:
Paraphrase 2-3 lines of the poem:
Subject:
Attitude:
Tone:
Symbol:
Shift:
Theme:

Shel Silverstein

Sheldon Allan "Shel" Silverstein (September 25, 1930 – May 10, 1999) was an American poet, singer-songwriter, cartoonist, screenwriter, and author of children's books. He styled himself as Uncle Shelby in some works. Translated into more than 30 languages, his books have sold over 20 million copies. He was the recipient of two Grammy Awards, as well as a Golden Globe and Academy Award nominee.

Recipe for a Hippopotamus Sandwich
A hippo sandwich is easy to make.
All you do is simply take
One slice of bread,
One slice of cake,
Some mayonnaise
One onion ring,
One hippopotamus
One piece of string,
A dash of pepper -
That ought to do it.
And now comes the problem…
Biting into it!

The Unicorn

A long time ago, when the earth was green
and there was more kinds of animals than you've ever seen,
and they run around free while the world was bein' born,
and the lovliest of all was the Unicorn.

There was green alligators and long-neck geese.
There was humpy bumpy camels and chimpanzees.

There was catsandratsandelephants, but sure as you're born
the lovliest of all was the Unicorn.

But the Lord seen some sinnin', and it caused him pain.
He says, 'Stand back, I'm gonna make it rain.'
He says, 'Hey Brother Noah, I'll tell ya whatcha do.
Go and build me a floatin' zoo.

And you take two alligators and a couple of geese,
two humpy bumpy camels and two chimpanzees.
Take two catsandratsandelephants, but sure as you're born,
Noah, don't you forget my Unicorn.'

Now Noah was there, he answered the callin'
and he finished up the ark just as the rain was fallin'.
He marched in the animals two by two,
and he called out as they went through,

'Hey Lord, I got your two alligators and your couple of geese,
your humpy bumpy camels and your chimpanzees.
Got your catsandratsandelephants - but Lord, I'm so forlorn
'cause I just don't see no Unicorn.'

Ol' Noah looked out through the drivin' rain
but the Unicorns were hidin', playin' silly games.
They were kickin' and splashin' in the misty morn,
oh them silly Unicorn.

The the goat started goatin', and the snake started snakin',
the elephant started elephantin', and the boat started shaking'.
The mouse started squeakin', and the lion started roarin',
and everyone's abourd but the Unicorn.

I mean the green alligators and the long-neck geese,
the humpy bumpy camels and the chimpanzees.
Noah cried, 'Close the door 'cause the rain is pourin' -
and we just can't wait for them Unicorn.'

Then the ark started movin', and it drifted with the tide,
and the Unicorns looked up from the rock and cried.
And the water come up and sort of floated them away -
that's why you've never seen a Unicorn to this day.

You'll see a lot of alligators and a whole mess of geese.
You'll see humpy bumpy camels and lots of chimpanzees.
You'll see catsandratsandelephants, but sure as you're born
you're never gonna see no Unicorn

Forgotten Language
Once I spoke the language of the flowers,
Once I understood each word the caterpillar said,
Once I smiled in secret at the gossip of the starlings,
And shared a conversation with the housefly
in my bed.
Once I heard and answered all the questions

of the crickets,
And joined the crying of each falling dying
flake of snow,
Once I spoke the language of the flowers. . . .
How did it go?
How did it go?

Journal #24: Write your own nonsensical poem

Using the techniques and elements you have learned in this class and you have seen reflected in the writing of Silverstein, write a short 6-8 line poem about something humorous or nonsensical.

DEVICES WORKSHEET

Device	Definition	Example	My example
Schemes of Construction – Parallelism	similarity of structure in a pair or series of related words, phrases, or clauses	"So Janey waited a bloom time, and a green time and an orange time." (Zora Neale Hurston, *Their Eyes Were Watching God*)	
Isocolon	is a scheme of parallel structure that occurs when the parallel elements are similar not only in grammatical structure but also in length	"His purpose was to impress the ignorant, to perplex the dubious, and to confound the scrupulous." (Hurston)	
Antithesis —	the juxtaposition of contrasting ideas, often in parallel structure.	Though studious, he was popular; though argumentative, he was modest; (Samuel Johnson).	
Schemes of unusual or inverted word order -- Anastrophe (an-ASS-tra-fee)	the inversion of natural word order, often with the purpose of surprising the reader	Ask not what your country can do for you, ask what you can do for your country." (John F. Kennedy)	
Parenthesis	insertion of some verbal unit in a position that interrupts the normal syntactical flow of the sentence	"Those two spots are among the darkest of our whole civilization— pardon me, our whole *culture* (an important distinction, I've heard), which might sound like a hoax, "(Ralph Ellison, *Invisible Man*)	
Schemes of Omission - Ellipsis -	deliberate omission of a word or of words that are readily implied by the context	"Twenty-two years old, weak, hot, frightened, not daring to acknowledge the fact that he didn't know who or what he was…with no past, no language," (Toni Morrison, Sula)	
Asyndeton (a SIN da ton) —	deliberate omission of conjunctions between a series of words, phrases, or clauses.	"I came, I saw, I conquered." (Julius Caesar)	
Polysyndeton —	deliberate use of many conjunctions (does not involve omission, but is grouped with its opposite, asyndeton)	"We lived and laughed and loved and left." (James Joyce, Finnegans Wake)	

Device	Definition	Example	My example
Schemes of Repetition Alliteration —	repetition of initial or medial consonants in two or more adjacent words.	"It was the **m**eanest **m**oment of eternity". (Zora Neale Hurston)	
Assonance -	the repetition of similar vowel sounds, preceded and followed by different consonants, in the stressed syllables of adjacent words.	Whales in the wake like capes and Alps/ Quaked the sick sea and snouted deep." (Dylan Thomas, "Ballad of the Long Legged Bait")	
(similarly) — Consonance	The repetition of the final consonant sound or sounds following different vowel sounds in proximal words.	"Blue with all malice, like a madman's fla**sh**; and thinly drawn with famishing for fle**sh**" (Wilfred Owens "Arms and the Boy).	
Anaphora	repetition of the same word or groups of words at the beginnings of successive phrases.	"We shall not flag or fail. We shall go on to the end. We shall fight in France" (Winston Churchill, 1940)	

Device	Definition	Example	My example
Epistrophe —	repetition of the same word or group of words at the ends of successive phrases.	"and that government of the people, by the people, for the people shall not perish from the earth." (Abraham Lincoln, Gettysburg Address)	
Epanalepsis (eh-puh-nuh-LEAP-siss) —	repetition of the same word or words at both beginning and ending of a phrase, clause, or sentence	Blood hath bought blood, and blows have answer'd blows:(William Shakespeare, King John)	
Anadiplosis (an-uh-dih-PLO-sis) —	repetition of the last word of one clause at the beginning of the following clause.	"The crime was common, common be the pain". (Alexander Pope, "Eloise to Abelard")	
Climax	arrangement of words, phrases, or clauses in an order of increasing importance.	". . . endurance produces character, and character produces hope, and hope does not disappoint us, because God's love has been poured into our hearts . .." (St. Paul, Romans)	
Antimetabole (an-tee-meh-TA-boe-lee)	repetition of words, in successive clauses, in reverse grammatical order.	"One should eat to live, not live to eat." (Moliere, L'Avare)	
Chiasmus (ki-AS-mus)	– (the "criss-cross") — reversal of grammatical structures in successive phrases or clauses	Exalts his enemies, his friends destroys." (John Dryden, "Absalom and Achitophel")	
Polyptoton (po-lyp-TO-ton) —	repetition of words derived from the same root.	"With eager feeding food doth choke the feeder." (Shakespeare's Richard II 2.1.37)	
Device	Definition	Example	My example
COMMON TROPES — *Deviation from the ordinary and principal meaning of a word*			
Metaphor -	implied comparison between two things of unlike nature	"The symbol of all our aspirations, one of the student leaders called her: the fruit of our struggle." (John Simpson, "Tianamen Square")	
Simile -	explicit comparison between two things of unlike nature, usually using "like" or "as"	"The night is bleeding like a cut." (Bono)	
Synecdoche (sih-NECK-duh-kee)	figure of speech in which a part stands for the whole	"Give us this day our daily bread." (Matthew, 6:11)	
Metonymy (me-TON-y-my) –	substitution of some attributive or suggestive word for what is actually meant.	The British crown has been plagued by scandal.	
Antanaclasis (AN-ta-na-CLA-sis)	repetition of a word or phrase whose meaning changes in the second instance. These are often "puns" as well.	Your argument is sound, nothing but sound." (Benjamin Franklin)	
Personification —	investing abstractions or inanimate objects with human qualities	"The night comes crawling in on all fours." (David Lowery)	
Hyperbole	— the use of exaggerated terms for the purpose of emphasis or heightened effect	"It rained for four years, eleven months, and two days." (Gabriel Garcia Marquez, One Hundred Years of Solitude)	
Litotes (LI-tuh-tees OR lie-TOE-tees) —	deliberate use of understatement	"It isn't very serious. I have this tiny little tumor on the brain." (Catcher in the Rye)	
Rhetorical question -	asking a question, not for the purpose of eliciting an answer but to assert or deny an answer implicitly	"Sir, at long last, have you left no sense of decency?" (Joseph Welch, The Army-McCarthy Hearings)	
Irony —	use of a word in such a way as to convey a meaning opposite to the literal meaning of the word	"This plan means that one generation pays for another. Now that's just dandy." (Huey P. Long)	
verbal irony –	when the words literally state the opposite of the writer's (or speaker's) meaning		

situational irony —ought to happen is not what does happen	when events turn out the opposite of what was expected; when what the characters and readers think		
(3) *dramatic irony* –	when facts or events are unknown to a character in a play or piece of fiction but known to the reader, audience, or other characters in the work.		
Onomatapoeia —	use of words whose sound echoes the sense	"…From the clamor and the clangor of the bells!" (Edgar Allan Poe, "The Bells")	
Oxymoron —	the joining of two terms which are ordinarily contradictory	"The unheard sounds came through, each melodic line existed of itself, stood out clearly from all the rest, said its piece, and waiting patiently for the other voices to speak." --Ralph Ellison, Invisible Man	
Paradox —	an apparently contradictory statement that nevertheless contains a measure of truth	"Whoever loses his life, shall find it." (Matthew, 16:25)	
Other Literary Analysis Terms			
allegory	The device of using character and/or story elements symbolically to represent an abstraction in addition to the literal meaning	Orwell's Animal Farm is an allegory on the brutality and dishonesty of the Soviet communist system.	
allusion	– A direct or indirect reference to something which is presumably commonly known, such as an event, book, etc. Allusions can be historical, literary, religious, topical, or mythical.	He was destined to fail; he always flew too close to the sun. (An allusion to the Greek myth *Icarus*.)	
analogy –	A similarity or comparison between two different things or the relationship between them	Getting politicians to agree is like herding cats."	
aphorism –	A terse statement of known authorship which expresses a general truth or a moral principle.	"A lie told often enough becomes the truth." ~ Vladimir Lenin	
atmosphere –	The emotional nod created by the entirety of a literary work, established by the setting and author's choice of objects that are described and can foreshadow events	"While I nodded, nearly napping, suddenly there came a tapping, As of someone gently rapping, rapping at my chamber door" – Poe, *The Raven*	
caricature –	A verbal description, the purpose of which is to exaggerate or distort, for comic effect or ridicule, a person's distinctive physical features or other characteristics	"Mr. Chadband is a large yellow man, with a fat smile, and a general appearance of having a good deal of train oil in his system." (Dickens, Bleak House)	
colloquial/colloquialism	– The use of slang or informalities in speech or writing	"But by-and-by pap got too handy with his hick'ry, and I couldn't stand it." (Mark Twain, Adventures of Huck Finn)	
conceit –	A fanciful expression, usually in the form of an metaphor or surprising analogy between seemingly dissimilar objects, usually used in poetry. A conceit displays intellectual cleverness as a result of the	Shakespeare's Sonnet 18: "Shall I compare thee to a summer's day?/Thou art more lovely and more temperate."	

	unusual comparison being made		
euphemism –	From the Greek for "good speech," euphemisms are a more agreeable or less offensive substitute for a generally unpleasant word or concept.	"For the time being," he explains, "it had been found necessary to make a readjustment of rations." (Orwell, Animal Farm)	
homily	– This term literally means "sermon," but more informally, it can include any serious talk, speech, or lecture involving moral or spiritual advice	Concerned parishioners brought Christmas baskets to our house. It was a humbling and difficult experience for my parents. The year before, my father had helped to distribute baskets to other poor people. Now it was our turn." (Father Bill Messenger to Eugene Parish, 1984)	
invective –	An emotionally violent, verbal denunciation or attack using strong, abusive language.	For example, in Henry IV, Part I, Prince Hal calls the large character of Falstaff "this sanguine coward, this bedpresser, this horseback breaker, this huge hill of flesh."	
mood –	The prevailing atmosphere or emotional aura of a work. Setting, tone, and events can affect the mood	"There was no moon, and everything beneath lay in misty darkness: not a light gleamed from any house, far or near all had been extinguished long ago:"(Emily Bronte, Wuthering Heights)	
Motif	Motif is an object or idea that repeats itself throughout a literary work	co-existence of good and evil in Harper Lee's "To Kill a Mocking Bird" is supported by several motifs. Lee strengthens the atmosphere by a motif of Gothic details i.e. recurrent images of gloomy and haunted settings,	
parody	– A work that closely imitates the style or content of another with the specific aim of comic effect and/or ridicule. It exploits peculiarities of an author's expression (propensity to use too many parentheses, certain favorite words, etc.).	Don Quixote" written by Miguel de Cervantes is a parody of romances written in his days. "Quixote" and his overweight sidekick "Sancho" delude themselves to think that they are knights of the medieval romances.	
satire –	A work that targets human vices and follies or social institutions and conventions for reform or ridicule.	"that for above seventy Moons past there have been two struggling Parties in this Empire, under the Names of Tramecksan and Slamecksan from the high and low Heels on their shoes, by which they distinguish themselves." (Jonathan Swift, Gulliver's Travels)	
symbol/symbolism –	Generally, anything that represents itself and stands for something else. Usually a symbol is something concrete -- such as an object, action, character, or scene – that represents something more abstract	"Ah Sunflower, weary of time, Who countest the steps of the sun; Seeking after that sweet golden clime Where the traveler's journey is done;" (William Blake, Ah Sunflower)	
natural symbols	are objects and occurrences from nature to symbolize ideas commonly associated with them	dawn symbolizing hope or a new beginning, a rose symbolizing love, a tree symbolizing knowledge.	
conventional symbols	are those that have been invested with meaning by a group	religious symbols such as a cross or Star of David; national symbols, such as a flag or an eagle; or group symbols, such as a skull and crossbones for pirates or the scale of justice for lawyers).	
literary symbols			

	are sometimes also conventional in the sense that they are found in a variety of works and are more generally recognized. However, a work's symbols may be more complicated.		
theme –	The central idea or message of a work, the insight it offers into life	Love and Friendship – Romeo and Juliet, Pride and Prejudice; War- Iliad, Farewell to Arms; Crime/Evil – Bleak House, Murders at Rue Morgue; Revenge – Hamlet, MacBeth, Count of Monte Cristo	
tone	– Similar to mood, tone describes the author's attitude toward his material, the audience, or both	"And the trees all died. They were orange trees. I don't know why they died, they just died." (David Barthelme, The School	

Appendix 1 – Story Elements

Elements of Plot:

- **Exposition:** Where the story's setting is presented, and the main character, our hero or protagonist, is introduced.
- **The inciting incident** is where the protagonist meets the villain or antagonist, and the ***conflict*** (see *appendix 2*) begins.
- **Rising Action:** This is where we start the journey with the protagonist. The protagonist stuffers small defeats, achieves small victories, and meets the other characters in the story that help move the journey forward.
- This all leads to the **darkness before the dawn.** This is the event right before the climax where we are left wording if it is possible for the protagonist will be able to overcome the conflict.
- **Climax:** This is the pivotal moment of the story where we learn who succeeds in the conflict, the protagonist or the villain/point of conflict.
- **Falling action:** this is what happens right after the climax, and what happens as an immediate result of the climax.
- **Resolution:** the ending of the story, what happens to the protagonist now that the conflict has ended.

Setting

The setting of a novel encompasses a number of different, but linked, elements:
   * time - day or night; summer or winter; the historical period (an actual date)
   * place - inside or outside; country or city; specific town and country; real or fictional
   * social - the minor characters who take little part in advancing the plot, but whose presence contributes to the realism of the novel
   * mood and atmosphere - eerie; dangerous; menacing; tense; threatening; relaxing; nostalgic; happy; light-hearted etc.
Setting is all the details of the time and place in which the story occurs.

Characters:
Stories have several different types of characters in them. Characters are either major or minor and either static (unchanging) or dynamic (changing). The character who dominates the story is the major character. This is the protagonist, the character that the reader or audience empathizes with.

 The antagonist in a work of fiction is the character who opposes the hero, or protagonist. The antagonist, when there is one, provides the story's conflict. In addition to these characters, a writer can include:
- A round character - a major character in a work of fiction who encounters conflict and is changed by it. They are also known as "dynamic characters." The protagonist is usually a round character.
- Flat characters - minor characters in a work of fiction who do not undergo substantial change or growth in the course of a story. They may also be called "static characters" and usually support a major character.
- Finally, a **Foil** is a character that is used to enhance another character through contrast. Cinderella's grace and beauty as opposed to her nasty, self-centered stepsisters is one clear illustration of a foil many may recall from childhood.
Narrative does not have to have all of these characters, but most good stories have them.

Appendix 2 – Conflict Information

In a literature, when something exciting happens in a story, it is usually bad. Until it does, we're not very interested. Tension might be the mother of fiction, but *problems* are the mother of tension.

In fiction, those problems are called conflict. More precisely, **conflict means thwarted, endangered, or opposing desire** – when a character wants something but something else gets in the way. Maybe the character wants a thing but cannot attain it. Maybe the character has something but is in danger of losing it. Maybe the character wants two things that are incompatible. Whatever its form, though, it gets our attention.

All conflict falls into two categories: internal and external.

- **Internal conflict** is when a character struggles with their own opposing desires or beliefs. It happens *within* them, and it drives their development as a character.
- **External conflict** sets a character against something or someone beyond their control. External forces stand in the way of a character's motivations and create tension as the character tries to reach their goals.

In any piece of literature, one, some, or all of the following conflicts might occur:

1. *Character vs. Self*
This is an internal conflict, meaning that the opposition the character faces is coming from within. This may entail a struggle to discern what the moral or "right" choice is, or it may also encompass mental health struggles.

2. *Character vs. Character*
This is a common type of external conflict in which one character's needs or wants are at odds with another's. A character conflict can be depicted as a straightforward fist fight, or as intricate and nuanced as the ongoing struggle for power in Shakespeare's MacBeth.

3. *Character vs. Nature*
In a nature conflict, a character is set in opposition to nature in external conflict. This can mean the weather, the wilderness, or a natural disaster. For example, in Ernest Hemingway's The Old Man and the Sea, the main character, Santiago finally manages to reel in a fish after months and months of bad luck. He fends off sharks, who are trying to steal his prized catch, but eventually they eat the fish—leaving Santiago with only a carcass. This is the essence of the man versus nature conflict: man struggles with human emotions, while nature charges forth undeterred.

4. *Character vs. Supernatural or Fate*
Pitting characters against phenomena like ghosts, gods, or monsters raises the stakes of a conflict by creating an unequal playing field. Supernatural conflict also covers characters, like Harry Potter or the tragic Odysseus, who have a fate or destiny and struggle to accept the sacrifices that come along with it. This type of conflict can be external or internal.

5. *Character vs. Technology*
In this case, a character is in external conflict with some kind of technology. Think of the tale of John Henry, the African American folk hero. In American folklore, Henry was a former slave who worked as a steel-driver on the rail line. To prove his superiority over new technology, he raced a steam-powered rock drilling machine and won. However, he suffered a heart attack after winning the race.

6. *Character vs. Society*
A character vs. society conflict is an external conflict that occurs in literature when the protagonist is placed in opposition with society, the government, or a cultural tradition or societal norm of some kind. Characters may be motivated to take action against their society by a need to survive, a moral sense of right and wrong, or a desire for happiness, freedom, justice, or love.

Appendix 3 – Grading rubric for essays

Rubric Area information:

Focus/Content/– meets paper requirements set by paper assignment; developed thesis; ideas tied to your thesis and reflect on your core topic; paragraphs/ideas are focused on topic/thesis and don't go off track. Thesis and topic are appropriate for the paper assignment. Paper employs critical thought and evaluation of ideas; it does not contain logical fallacies or rely on reader assumptions. Topic is approached with insight and draws strong conclusions.

Organization: Organization guides the reader from one idea, sentence, or paragraph to the next; language moves your essay and helps avoid jumpiness in writing through the use of transitions. Your overall ideas have logical flow; you keep like ideas together in your writing. The paper contains an introduction with a specific, unified thesis, body paragraphs, and a conclusion. Paper ideas follows the presentation of the thesis. Each body paragraph serves a purpose and contains requisite topic sentences, evidence, and explanations for the thesis.

Support/Development – Argument is well presented with adequate support. Appropriate use of source material/quotes through the use of textual evidence to prove thesis. Insightful use of metacommentary (explanation of the source material in the context of your essay) and quote integration (no floating quotes). Provides elaboration of ideas by definition, importance, what the reader should understand from your examples/ideas, and why this evidence supports the thesis. Details should highlight logical and analytical thinking in response to sources and in development of ideas; use examples and ideas for specific details; paper meets evidence requirements set forth in class.

Style/Voice/Tone/ Grammar/Proofreading – Paper avoids redundancy, vague wording or vague development of ideas. Use of specific language, nouns, verbs, and ideas and college-level vocabulary; answering questions instead of asking them. Writer uses more formal tone in writing and avoid slang and does not use "you" or "I" language. Paper avoids passive voice, announcement language, and awkward/convoluted sentencing; use of strong sentence variation for strong written structure; sentences logically convey writer's meaning. Proper comma usage; paper avoids comma splices/run-ons and sentence fragments. Writing uses correct agreement and tense usage, correct spelling and wording, and proper grammar, mechanics, and punctuation usage overall. Writing has no typos; appropriate capitalization, use of abbreviations, titles, and numbering; meets requirements set forth in class.

Formatting/Research/ MLA- Paper includes proper use of quotation marks and commas/periods, strong quote integration and formatting of quotes as necessary, correct in-text citations, and correct bibliographic "Works Cited" page formatting. Paper proper paragraphing with a title, first line indents, and correct margins with name and page number on each page; meets MLA and requirements set forth in class.

Appendix 4 – Answer for Journal Activities

Journal #1: Paradox intro

I. Scientists have discovered time travel. John goes back in time to 1900 and meets his great-grandfather as a young child. John invites the boy to see the circus. Unfortunately, there's an accident at the circus which paralyzes the boy from his neck down. What is the paradox? *That if he grandfather can't have children, then John is never born.*

2. Leslie tells her friends at school that she lost her cell phone at the basketball game that afternoon. "If you find it, call or text me." What is the paradox? *That she can't accept calls or texts if she doesn't have her phone.*

Journal #2: Native Myths

1. Explain what you can infer about the place of dreams in Native American Culture from the excerpt from "The Earth on Turtle's Back." *ANSWERS MAY VARY – that dreams have power*
   a. Identify the main characters of this myth. *Chief, Sky woman (his wife), water birds, Tiny Muskrat, Great Turtle*
   b. What conflicts can you identify? *ANSWERS MAY VARY – Man vs nature, man vs fate*
2. What does the excerpt from "When Grizzles Walked Upright" tell you about the beliefs of Native Americans regarding taking responsibility for one's actions? *ANSWERS MAY VARY – that one must understand the consequences of one's actions.*
   a. Describe the setting of this myth and possible conflicts – *the mountains, Mt Shasta, and ANSWERS MAY VARY – Man vs nature, man vs fate*
3. What does the excerpt from "The Navajo Origin Legend" tell you about why the Navajo believed the wind was what gave life to people? *ANSWERS MAY VARY – that the wind holds the power of the gods*
   a. What is the outcome of this myth? *ANSWERS MAY VARY – the creation of the first man and woman on earth*
   b. What conflicts led to this outcome? *ANSWERS MAY VARY – Man vs nature, man vs fate*

Journal # 3: Jonathan Edwards

1. Consider your prior knowledge of Puritan life and belief systems. In what ways does Edwards' sermon model Puritan beliefs? *ANSWERS MAY VARY - of being strict in religious discipline, believed that God has the power for everything, uncompromising when it came to their religion and beliefs.*
2. What are the prominent themes communicated by the images and analogies that Edwards uses? *ANSWERS MAY VARY - Divine Justice, God's Judgement, the unrepentant man is subject to God's wrath.*
3. How does Edwards use rhetorical elements in the sermon? Use the devices worksheet in this text to help you identify the devices used in the sermon. ? *ANSWERS MAY VARY – allusions to hell-- horrors of hell by referencing common terms to make the listener have a visual connection to hell. "The pit is prepared, the fire made ready." Similes -- burns like fire. Personification -- A boundless duration before you, which will swallow up you thought -- to show God's anger towards humans.*

Journal #4: Anne Bradstreet
1. What are some examples of plain language in the poem? *ANSWERS MAY VARY – man, woman, we, gold . . .*
2. Why do you think she uses this type of language? *ANSWERS MAY VARY*
3. What examples of language in the poem show more dynamic language usage? Why does it seem to stand out? *ANSWERS MAY VARY – rivers cannot quench; from the give recompense . . . because these elements are more dynamic and flowery than the plain language, and not used as much, so when it is used, it stands out.*
4. Using the Devices worksheet, identify some of the devices she uses in her poem. *ANSWERS MAY VARY – metaphor (mines of gold), hyperbole (riches that the East doth hold)*

Journal #5 Thomas Paine

Part ONE: Identify the type(s) of appeal used and the effect he hopes it will have on his audience:

1. Tyranny, like hell, is not easily conquered; yet we have this consolation with us, that the harder the conflict, the more glorious the triumph. What we obtain, too cheap, we esteem too lightly:--'Tis dearness only that gives every thing its value. *Logical appeal, logos, logical chain of thoughts, and Answers may vary*

2. I turn with the warm ardour of a friend to those who have nobly stood yet determined to stand the matter out; I call not upon a few, but upon all; not on THIS state or THAT truth but on EVERY state; *Emotional appeal, pathos, appealing to warm feelings and nobility, and Answers may vary*

3. Not all the treasures of the world, is far as I believe, could have induced me to support an offensive war, for I think it murder; But if a thief break into my house, burn and destroy my property, and kill or threaten to kill me, or those that are in it, and to "bind me in all cases whatsoever," to his absolute will, am I to suffer it? What signifies it to me, whether he who does it, is a king or a common man; my countryman or not my countryman; whether it is done by an individual villain, or an army of them? If we reason to the root of things we shall find no difference; neither can any just cause be assigned why we should punish in the one case, and pardon in the other . . . *Logical Appeal, logos – logical chain of events, and Answers may vary*

Part TWO: Look back at the passages and identify any "charged" language- any words or language that is used solely to elicit a strong emotional response from the reader, or words that have an association that can affect the reader. Then, using the Devices worksheet, identify rhetorical devices Paine uses in his writing. *Answers may vary – "slavery," "thief" "villain," "Tyranny, like hell," "glorious triumph," "not infested . . . "*

Journal #6 - Revolution and Kipling

Answer the following question in a short paragraph:

What is Kipling's point of view about the American Revolution in this part of the poem? Cite specific examples. Make a comment about why you think the poem is titled the way it is.
Answers may vary; That the colonists waited until they were established on the new land to decide to seek their freedom, that they used the British to be settled before making their Revolution; the title means that it was a rebellion, like a child against a parent, rather than a revolution against an oppressive government.

Journal #7 - Irving:

1. What mood does the setting of this story create? *Somber, dark, isolated, dreamy . . . are some examples*
2. Who do the villagers believe the headless horseman is? How did he lose his head? *Hessian soldier that had his head blown off during the American Revolution*
3. What do the villagers think he is doing out at night? *Searching for his head before sunlight.*
4. Where does Ichabod Crane live? Why does he need to be able to have all of his belongings in a small bundle? *Ichabod Crane lives in one of the farm houses, and he needs to be able to carry all his items in a small bundle because he travels a lot.*
5.   Why do the women in the countryside think he is an important person? How do the mothers treat him as a result? How do the younger girls respond to him? *Schoolmasters were generally more educated than anyone else. Therefore, they were thought to be superior in their tastes and habits. The mothers, therefore, treated him to their finest food and nicest china in an attempt to show him their own refinement. Ichabod spent a great deal of time with the girls, impressing them and making the other boys jealous with his "superior elegance and way of talking."*
6. What approach does Brom Bones (Brom Van Brunt) want to take when he discovers Ichabod is interested in Katrina? Why can't he do that? *Brom wants to hurt him; Ichabod refused to fight (he'd obviously lose)*
7. Contrast Ichabod Crane and Brom Bones. How are they different in physical appearance? How are their actions different? What would have made Katrina attracted to each of them? *Answers may vary – Ichabod takes care*

in his appearance, is more slender and less apt at fighting than Brom. Brom represents strength and Ichabod represents refinery for Katrina . . .

8. What are two things Brom Bones does to get back at Ichabod for trying to steal Katrina? *ridicules, jokes and make fun of him in front of Katrina*

9. What evidence is there that Ichabod Crane had an active imagination? *Answers may vary – Whenever he went in the forest, he would get worried and spooked by his own imagination . . .*

10. What mood is Ichabod in when he leaves Katrina's house that night? What evidence is there of his mood? What speculation does the author make as to what happened? *he is scared; happy for a good night, but quiet, and second guessing his relationship, dismal and disheartened by that*

11. What logical explanation is there for three of the things Ichabod sees or hears when he is near the old, large tree? *whistle: blast of wind; sees white: bark came off tree; groan: branches rubbing against one another*

12. When Ichabod sees something huge and black by the brook, why doesn't he turn and run away? What two things does he do instead? What four traces of the chase do the searchers find the next day? *because he thinks it is too late and demanded "Who are you?" – They find a smashed pumpkin, Ichabod laying on the floor, horse tracks and the horse.*

13. What makes it seem that Brom Bones knew something about what happened that night? *He has a hearty laugh and a knowing look.*

14. What did the people of the town believe about what happened that night? *That the Headless Horseman killed Ichabod.*

Journal #8 The Raven

Stanza 1.
1. What was the speaker doing? What condition was he in? *by himself, reading books*
2. What did he hear? *A knock at his door.*

Stanza 2.
1. What does the speaker give us to see in the second line? What is the speaker wishing for? *The idea of ghosts, wishing to feel better over losing his love.*
2. What had he been doing with his books? Why? *Trying to read, as an escape from his sorrow.*
3. Who is Lenore? *A beautiful woman he loved.*
4. What does the last line mean? *Nameless means no longer of this world, dead.*

Stanza 3.
1. What vision does the speaker give in the first line? How does he make it seem eerie? *Purple curtains, words like sad and uncertain*
2. What does he say in the second line? What seems to be happening to him? *Thrilled with terrors, he is afraid.*
3. What type of state does he seem to be going into? Why? *A state of shock or surprise or disbelief, thinking he's seeing ghosts. Trying to convince himself it's a real person at the door.*

Stanza 4.
1. Does he open the door before or after he speaks? *After.*
2. What does he find when he opens the door? *Nothing but darkness*

Stanza 5.
1. Does he close the door or keep it open? What does he see? *Keeps it open, sees only darkness.*
2. What is the darkness like? How does it make him feel? What does he say? *Dreamlike, eerie, whispers Lenore.*
3. What does he hear? Does he really hear something or is it his imagination? *Name echoed back, probably imagination.*

Stanza 7.
1. He has shut the door and moved to the window, how does he open the window? *Flings it open, panicked.*
2. What does he find? *A raven.*
3. How does the speaker say the Raven acted in lines three and four? *Stately, like a lord or lady.*
4. What does the Raven do? *Sits over his door and watches him.*

Stanza 8.
1. What does the bird do for the speaker in the first line? How is this ironic? *Beguiles him – birds don't act consciously this way – he is beguiling himself.*
2. Where does the speaker think the bird has come from? Why? *From Hell – "Night's shore" is a reference to the edges of Hell's river Styx.*
3. What does the speaker ask the bird? What does the bird reply? *He asks the bird who he is, the raven responds Nevermore – which was what the speaker called Lenore earlier in the poem.*

Stanza 9.
1. How does the speaker feel about the Raven in his chamber?
2. Does he think that the bird's presence has any significance? Why/why not?

Stanza 9
1. Has the Raven moved since entering the house? How do you know (L.1 and L.3.)?
2. What does the speaker believe the bird will do?
3. When does he believe that the bird will leave? What does the bird say?

Stanza 10
1. What word does the speaker wish to be the last spoken between him and the bird?
2. Where does he tell the bird to go?
3. What is a black plume?
4. What does the speaker imply when he tells the Raven to take its beak from his heart? How does the speaker feel about the Raven at this point?

Stanza 11.
1. In the last stanza, where is the bird? What eerie vision does the speaker give in lines three & four?
2. When else in the poem did he speak of shadows?
3. Who or what might the Raven symbolize?
4. What does it mean when the speaker says that the shadow on the floor shall be lifted nevermore? (He will always carry his guilt/mourning.)
5. Who says nevermore?
6. What conclusions can we draw about what effects the Raven has had on the speaker?

Review and Conclusion questions:
6. Why did Poe use a Raven instead of another bird? What is the symbol of a Raven?
7. When did the speaker become paranoid? Why?
8. What movies/TV programs can you think of when a person becomes scared of something outside?
9. Why would Lenore be at his door if she died? How do you think she died?
10. W here does the speaker's imagination take control of his mind?

Journal #9: Hiawatha and Old Ironsides:

Respond to the following questions:
Song of Hiawatha:

4. What is the effect of rhythm in the poem Song of Hiawatha on the reader? *Answers may vary – sounds like drums or is regular and sets a beat to the poem*
5. What is the effect of repetition on the reader? *Emphasizes meaning of repeated words, adds to rhythmic nature of poem*
6. Why do you think the poet might have used unusual word order? *Answers may vary – to create rhythm, to mimic the tribal songs of Native peoples, to start each line with its own important element*

Old Ironsides:
3. Identify two lines in the poem that show the action in this battle were violent. *Answers may vary*
4. What is the speaker's overall attitude about the demise of the ship? *The speaker is sad about the ship being scrapped, the speaker suggests that instead of tearing it apart, it should be permitted to sink to the bottom of the sea*

Journal #10 – Paradox part 2

Write Y in the blank of each paradox. Write N in the blank if it is not a paradox.

___Y____ I know that I know nothing.
____N_____ He was too tired to go to sleep.
____Y____ I always lie.
_____Y____ Call me if you find my phone.
____N_____ She'll be your friend through thick and thin.

Write a T for the paradoxes that can be true. Write an F for those that cannot be true.

___T_____ You have to spend money to save money.
____T_____ Deep down inside, he's a very shallow person.
___T_____ Sometimes you must be cruel to be kind.
____F_____ No one goes to that movie theater; it's too crowded.
___F ____ "I can resist anything but temptation." - Oscar Wilde

Explain why each statement below is a paradox.

1. Don't go into the water until you know how to swim. *You have to go into water to learn to swim.*
2. Rule #10: Ignore all rules. *Ignoring all the rules means ignoring rule 10.*
3. If you do not have an Internet connection, go to this website for help. *You have to have internet to go to the website.*

Journal #11: Dickenson:
Part 1: Select one of Dickenson's poems. Identify and label the poem's rhyme scheme with the appropriate lettering. – *Answers may vary*

Part 2: Identify Metaphorical and hidden deeper meanings of *Because I could Not Stop for Death*:
1. What is the overall Metaphorical meaning of the poem*? Answers may vary – examples include: The drive symbolizes her leaving life. She progresses from childhood, maturity (the "gazing grain" is ripe) and the setting (dying) sun to her grave. The children are presented as active in their leisure ("strove"). The images of children and grain suggest futurity, that is, they have a future; they also depict the progress of human life*
2. What is the deeper allegorical meaning of the following lines?
    a. We passed the school where Children strove   At Recess – in the ring: *The passage of childhood, innocence, something she is outside of*
    b. We passed the Fields of Grazing Grain: *the future/ they have a future*
    c. We passed the Setting Sun: *the end of the cycle of life*
    d. Or rather – He passed Us : *passing out of time and into eternity*

Journal # 12 Thoreau

1. What might it mean to live "deliberately"?
_____

2. What might be several of the "essential facts" about life that Thoreau wants to "front" (or confront)?
_____

3. What do you think he means when he says he "did not wish to practice resignation"?
_____

4. What does "suck out all the marrow of life" mean to you?
_____

5. What does it mean to "drive life into a corner and reduce it to its lowest terms"?

_____

6. What might this sentence tell us about Thoreau's religious belief?

Journal #13: Model Writing

Mock Writing based on Dickenson or Thoreau. Start with the phrase "There's a certain Slant of light, _____" OR "I went to the woods because I wished to live_____" -- fill in the blank. Then finish the paragraph stanza with a description of that fits the word/phrase you selected. *Answers may vary. Grade on effort.*

Journal #14: Uncle Tom's Cabin:
Answers may vary
1. Why does George say he wishes he had never seen Eliza? *If he had never seen Eliza, they never would have married or had Harry. He wouldn't be facing separation from Eliza or Harry.*
2. What does George mean when he says "a sword will pierce through your soul for every good and pleasant thing your child is or has…"? *Every good trait of Harry's will make him more valuable and more likely to be sold, which will break Eliza's heart.*
3. Why does Eliza turn pale and gasp for breath? *She knows George is right and she could lose Harry at any time.*

Journal #15 Whitman:
1.   Identify Rhetorical Elements in "O Captain, My Captain!" – use the Devices worksheet to help you.
        Answer the following questions about "O Captain, My Captain!"
        a.   "O Captain! My Captain!" was written just after the end of the Civil War. The speaker's description of a captain who dies most likely refers to who? *Abraham Lincoln*
        b.   The use of the phrase "my Captain" in the title and throughout the poem suggests that the speaker is what? *Loyal to the captain.*
        c.   Which phrase suggests that the ship has survived a difficult situation? *Our fearful Trip*
        d.   What does the ship in the poem symbolize? *The United States*
        e.   The tone in the third stanza of "O Captian! My Captain" is best described as what? *Mournful*
        f.   In line 21 the speaker says, "the ship is anchor'd safe and sound." The idea of safety is ironic, or unexpected because . . . ? *The captain is dead on the deck,*

    2. In *Song of Myself*, What does Whitman mean when he says, "If you want me again, look for me under your boot-soles"?
        1.   His poetry is everywhere.
        2.   He is a "grass-roots" poet.
        3.   He is a common man, just like anyone else.
        4.   *all of the above*
        5.   none of the above

In Song of Myself,
  3. Walt Whitman expresses his identification with
        1.   death
        2.   *nature*
        3.   his mother
        4.   time
        5.   none of the above

    4.   Who does the narrator celebrate and sing? *I celebrate myself and sing myself*
    5.   What is an example of imagery? An example of a figure of speech? Imagery example: grass is a symbol of hope, growth, and death; imagery example: journey. Figure of speech example: alliteration, rhetorical questions, rhyming scheme

Journal #16 Paradox part 3:

Explain why each is a paradox.

1) Robert Frost, "The Tuft of Flowers"
"Men work together," I told him from the heart,
"Whether they work together or apart."
Answer: Since together and apart are opposites of each other, it seems impossible to work together and apart at the same time

2) Oscar Wilde, "Lady Windemere's Fan"
I can resist everything except temptation.
Answer: If you can resist everything, then that should include temptation. Also, the only thing that humans resist is temptation, so he actually resists nothing

3) Emily Dickinson, "Poems, Series 2
I'm nobody! Who are you?
Are you nobody, too?
Answer: She can't be nobody, since she is somebody

Journal #17: Realism

Realism diary entries – from the point of view of either Huck Finn or Chief Joseph, write 2-3 diary entries that shows the realism of the time, setting, and events. *Answers may vary. Grade on effort*

Journal #18 The Last Leaf Comprehension Questions
1.   How is pneumonia described in the story?
It is described as an "unseen stranger"
Touches with icy fingers-smiting victims by scores

2.   What does the doctor mean by "lining up on the side of the undertaker?"
Accepting death- welcoming it
Giving up- wanting to die

3.   What comparisons describe Johnsy's appearance and feelings?
"Like a fallen statue" meaning pale and still as a marble
"Like those poor, tired leaves" meaning death floating downward

4.   Describe Mr. Behrman's relationship with Sue and Johnsy.
He is fond of them, and feels protective of them.

5.   Why does Sue call the leaf that Mr. Behrman painted his "masterpiece?"
The leaf was painted so well that Johnsy was convinced it was alive- the leaf saved her life. It was apparently the finest piece of work that Behrman ever painted.

6.   What was the twist in the story?
Behrman died without ever realizing he painted his "masterpiece" – which he strived to create for years.
7. Answer May Vary.

Journal #19: Prufrock

"The Love Song of J. Alfred Prufrock": Answers may vary	Guiding Questions
1) Lines 1-12	1) Who is the speaker of the poem and to whom is the poem addressed? *To himself; stream of consciousness, his mind wanders*
2) Lines 1-14	2) Where is the speaker? Describe the time of day, place, etc. What parts of the poem support your answer? *His residence – "cheap hotels and sawdust restaurants . . ."*
3) Lines 1-14	3) Identify two SIMILES in the opening stanza. What do these similes suggest about what is being compared to something else? *Like a patient etherized upon a table" and "Streets that follow like a tedious argument." Both of these similes have negative connotations. To be etherized is to be anesthetized, unaware of one's environment, as the individual is as if*

	dead, hence unaware of the world. To compare the streets to a "tedious argument" invokes ideas of boredom and irritation.
4) Lines 13-14	**4) What room is the speaker describing?** *room where "women come and go / Talking of Michelanglo" would be one where the women have leisure time to talk about art. This implies they are educated and belong to a similar social circle*
5) Lines 15-22	**5) Identify the primary METAPHOR in this stanza. In other words, to what does the poet indirectly liken the yellow fog? Note specific elements/words from the poem to support your answer.** *equating the "yellow fog" with a cat "that rubs its muzzle.../Licked its tongue"..."Slipped by the terrace, made a sudden leap / [and] Curled once about the house, and fell asleep*
6) Lines 23-34	**6) What is the primary argument of this stanza? Sum up the argument in one sentence.** *that there is always time for all the things one wants or wishes for in life*
7) Lines 37-48	**7) What is the speaker's emotional state at this point in the poem? What are his primary concerns?** *anxiety; he believes any action on his part with reverberate throughout the universe. His primary concern is with how people with perceive his appearance, that he is growing old with a 'bald spot."*
8) Line 51	**8) What does the speaker mean in line 51 to "measure out in coffee spoons"?** *To measure out one's life with coffee spoons indicates that his life is shallow and small, devoid of deep, satisfying experiences.*
9) Lines 49-69	**9) Identify the poem's use of REPETITION? What effect does repetition have on the poem's meaning?** *Prufrock's indecisiveness because he needs to repeat things to himself to come up with a decision. However, by repeating the rhetorical question, the effect is multiplied, magnifying his inability to make up his mind and his lack of confidence in himself*
10) Lines 49-69	**10) What is the speaker's TONE at this point in the poem? Support with text.** one of pessimism and inadequacy. *He takes an empirical, scientific approach to both others, whom he views as having "arms that are braceleted*
11) Line 66	12) **Re-read line 66. What stands out about the act of digressing?** *technique of stream of consciousness is used throughout the poem, ironically here Prufock acknowledges the act when he refers to the perfume, but in reality, he has done nothing but digress*
12) Lines 75-86	12) **Do you think the speaker himself is digressing? Identify parts of the poem to support your answer.** *Prufrock jumps from one topic to another without logical transitions. For example, he thinks about the woman to whom he will propose and how he will accomplish this; at the same time he anticipates rejection*
14) Lines 90-98	**14) Describe the speaker's relationship to speaking itself? Is he effective at expressing himself and/or telling a story? Why or why not?** *inarticulate and states, "It is impossible to say just what I mean." This is further supported in the manner he disassociates his actions,*

15) Lines 120-125	15) Has the speaker finally admitted his primary concern? What effect does "growing old" have on the speaker's socializing? *reflects his fear of death. He is under the delusion that he can hold back time, if he "wear[s] the bottom of [his] trousers rolled" or parts his "hair behind." In his mind, these actions will allow him to keep socializing.*
16) Lines 129-131	16) What is the speaker's final tone? Explain. *evoke a deep sadness, for Prufrock believes that connecting with people, awakening to a life force, means death. This is an irreconcilable paradox that is the foundation of his existential angst.*

Journal #20 Modern Poetry:

Student responses and writing may vary. Grade on effort.

Journal #21: Frost

1. What is the rhyme scheme? – mark it on the poems. *Road*: ABAAB, *Wall*: Blank verse

Answers may vary:

2. What decision does the speaker have to make in *The Road not Taken*? To make the same choice that everyone else does (peer pressure), or to have their own mind/make a choice others might not.

3. Infer the season in both poems. How do you know? *Road*: Autumn *Wall*: Spring

4. Explain why the reader doubts he'll ever come back to travel the first road in *the Road Not Taken*. *He will never have the chance to double back – the road he picks will never lead back to this spot – you can't go back in time to remanke a decision.*

5. Describe the conflict the speaker feels in both *The Road not Taken* and *The Mending Wall*. *Road: to succumb to peer pressure or make their own decision. Wall: to reach out to the neighbor and have a wide open land, or to make sure that everyone knows what one's boundaries are.*

Journal #22: Hughes/Harlem Renaissance
Answers will vary. Grade on effort

Journal #23: Angelou – *answers may vary*
Title: *explains why a caged bird is singing – maybe it is happy where it is. Maybe it feels safer in its cage.*
Paraphrase 2-3 lines of the poem: example: *lines 8-10: But the bird walking around its cage can't see past its anger at being caged up. He can't fly, so he sings instead.*
Subject*: the difference between the caged bird and the free bird;*
Attitude: *heartbroken about the condition of the caged bird*
Tone: *For the free bird, good tone words might be: free, dares, soft, sighing, fat, bright*
Symbol: *Free bird, caged bird*
Shift: *shifts in stanzas three and six. While the other stanzas describe what the birds are doing, stanzas three and six describe why the caged bird sings*
Theme: *examples - Physical imprisonment leads to mentally seeking freedom; Being denied what others have make a person understand the things better*

Journal #24: Write your own nonsensical poem

Using the techniques and elements you have learned in this class and you have seen reflected in the writing of Silverstein, write a short 6-8 line poem about something humorous or nonsensical. *Answers may vary. Graded on effort.*

Appendix 5 -- Added Activities for your student:

If you feel your students needs more of a challenge or additional work for a more advanced class, feel free to add in these assignments and activities:

Read additional literature by one of the authors we have read and write a one paragraph summary.

Create art, collages, or drawings based on any of the readings.

Watch any one of the following movies based in American Literature and write a one paragraph summary (if there is another movie you are familiar with that reflects American literature and you would like to read it, feel free!):

To kill a Mockingbird

The Princess Bride

Lord of the Flies

Little Women

DaVinci Code

Of Mice and Men

Grapes of Wrath

Adventures of Huck Finn

Tom Sawyer

Dead Poets Society

Jurassic Park

The Crucible

Old Man and the Sea

Farewell to Arms

For Whom the Bell Tolls

Moby Dick

In the Heart of the Sea

Legends of the Fall

The House of Usher

The Last of the Mohicans

The Great Gatsby

To Kill a Mockingbird

The Pit and the Pendulum

Fahrenheit 451

Beloved

Their Eyes were Watching God

The Color Purple

Old Yeller

The Wizard of Oz

Appendix 6 – Final Quiz and answer key:

Answer Key:

<u>American Literature Final</u>   Name: _____ /score_____/40

Match the quote with the correct text (1 pt each):

1. moving tense/ unheeded/ to gong clang/s siren howls/ and wheels rumbling/through/ the dark city.

    a. Man with the Hoe
    b. *The Great Figure*
    c. Love Song of J Alfred Prufrock
    d. The Road not Taken

2. Streets that follow like a tedious argument/ Of insidious intent/To lead you to an overwhelming question….

Oh, do not ask, "What is it?"/Let us go and make our visit.

    a. This is just to say
    b. Mending Wall
    c. Man with the Hoe
    d. *Love Song of J Alfred Prufrock*

3. My soul has grown deep like the rivers.
    a. The Weary Blues
    b. Mending Wall
    c. Still I Rise
    d. *The Negro Speaks of Rivers*

4. . In Poe's "The Raven," the raven represents what?
    a. the lost Lenore
    b. *his madness over his inability to cope with his loss*
    c. his sadness over losing his loved one
    d. a ghost or spectre

5. I took the one less traveled by,
And that has made all the difference.
    a. Mending Wall
    b. The Road not Taken
    c. This is just to say
    d. Love Song of J Alfred Prufrock

6. Read the following sentence from The Grapes of Wrath by John Steinbeck:

The tractors came over the roads and into the fields, great crawlers moving like insects, having the incredible strength of insects. They crawled over the ground, laying the track and rolling on it and picking it up.

Which statement best describes the effect of the simile on the excerpt's meaning?

   a. It gives tractors human qualities to show how busy they are.
   b. *It compares tractors to insects to convey their unstoppable force.*
   c. It uses the term "great crawlers" to indicate that the tractors couldn't go far.
   d. It links tractors to flies to show how quickly the tractors move.

7. One of the many themes found in the novel, The Scarlet Letter, is:

   1. Black vs. White
   2. Man vs. Nature
   3. *Punishment vs. Forgiveness*
   4. True friendship never fails

8. Which of the following is a definition of Transcendentalism:

   a. *A movement that promoted freedom, individuality, and a community with nature*

   b. An idea that showed how industrialism was important to the individual

   c. A book that a man wrote about how to "suck all the marrow out of life"

   d. A belief that all men are created inherently evil and need civilization

9. Walt Whitman's "Oh Captain, My Captain" focuses on which significant event:

   a. The death of his wife

   b. *The death of Abraham Lincoln*

   c. The end of the Civil War

   d. The death of his son

10. The Grapes of Wrath follows which family?

   1. *The Joad Family*
   2. The Toad Family
   3. The Jones Family
   4. The Martin Family

Respond to the following questions (2 points each):

11. List three literary devices that show imagery in a text: *symbol, motif, caricature, allegory*

12. List 3 ways "Hiawatha" can be described as a Romantic poem: *connection to nature, appeal to Native culture, noble savage, focus on emotions*

13. Provide an example of paradox in writing: *answers may vary*

14. List three elements of Romanticism: *connection with nature, rejecting civilization, reliance on emotions and intuition, connection to the natural man, Noble savage, respect for Native people, seeking the divine inside oneself.*

15. List three themes from *Old Man and the Sea*: *tenacity, defeat, the struggle of man vs nature, age, loneliness*

16: How does "Love Song of J Alfred Prufrock" reflect the Modern Era of writing? *Quest for understanding, free verse, stream of consciousness*

17. What do we call the minor genre in which Langston Hughes wrote? *Harlem Renaissance*

18. Which writer wrote in the Modern movement? *William Carlos Williams, T.S. Eliot*

19. What is the climax in *Jury of her Peers*? *That the bird is the evidence of her guilt*

20. What was your favorite piece we read this semester and why? *Answers may vary*

Match the quote with the correct text (2 pt each):

1. moving tense/ unheeded/ to gong clang/s siren howls/ and wheels rumbling/through/ the dark city.

- e. Man with the Hoe
- f. The Great Figure
- g. Love Song of J Alfred Prufrock
- h. The Road not Taken

2. Streets that follow like a tedious argument/ Of insidious intent/To lead you to an overwhelming question….

Oh, do not ask, "What is it?"/Let us go and make our visit.

- e. This is just to say
- f. Mending Wall
- g. Man with the Hoe
- h. Love Song of J Alfred Prufrock

3. My soul has grown deep like the rivers.
- e. The Weary Blues
- f. Mending Wall
- g. Still I Rise
- h. The Negro Speaks of Rivers

4. In Poe's "The Raven," the raven represents what?

a. the lost Lenore

b. his madness over his inability to cope with his loss

c. his sadness over losing his loved one

d. a ghost or spectre

5. I took the one less traveled by,
And that has made all the difference.
- e. Mending Wall
- f. The Road not Taken
- g. This is just to say
- h. Love Song of J Alfred Prufrock

6. Read the following sentence from The Grapes of Wrath by John Steinbeck:

The tractors came over the roads and into the fields, great crawlers moving like insects, having the incredible strength of insects. They crawled over the ground, laying the track and rolling on it and picking it up.

Which statement best describes the effect of the simile on the excerpt's meaning?

- e. It gives tractors human qualities to show how busy they are.
- f. It compares tractors to insects to convey their unstoppable force.
- g. It uses the term "great crawlers" to indicate that the tractors couldn't go far.
- h. It links tractors to flies to show how quickly the tractors move.

7. One of the many themes found in the novel, The Scarlet Letter, is:

1. Black vs. White
2. Man vs. Nature
3. Punishment vs. Forgiveness
4. True friendship never fails

8. Which of the following is a definition of Transcendentalism:

a. A movement that promoted freedom, individuality, and a community with nature

b. An idea that showed how industrialism was important to the individual

c. A book that a man wrote about how to "suck all the marrow out of life"

d. A belief that all men are created inherently evil and need civilization

9. Walt Whitman's "Oh Captain, My Captain" focuses on which significant event:

a. The death of his wife

b. The death of Abraham Lincoln

c. The end of the Civil War

d. The death of his son

10. The Grapes of Wrath follows which family?

1. The Joad Family
2. The Toad Family
3. The Jones Family
4. The Martin Family

Respond to the following questions (2 points each):

11. List three literary devices that show imagery in a text:

12. List 3 ways "Hiawatha" can be described as a Romantic poem:

13. Provide an example of paradox in writing:

14. List three elements of Romanticism:

15. List three themes from *Old Man and the Sea*:

16: How does "Love Song of J Alfred Prufrock" reflect the Modern Era of writing?

17. What do we call the minor genre in which Langston Hughes wrote?

18. Which writer wrote in the Realist movement?

19. What is the climax in *Jury of her Peers*?

20. What was your favorite piece we read this semester and why?

Appendix 7: American Literature Research Essay Outline and Information

Many individuals in history have had a major influence on American literature. Pick an author who has had a major impact and research him or her, examining the significance of his or her role.

Jonathan Edwards	Henry David Thoreau	Charlotte Perkins Gilman
William Bradford		Markham
Anne Bradstreet	Nathaniel Hawthorne	
Benjamin Franklin	Edgar Allan Poe	Robert Frost
• Thomas Paine	Walt Whitman	William Carlos Williams
Washington Irving	Emily Dickinson	T.S. Eliot
Oliver Wendell Holmes		Langston Hughes John Steinbeck
• Henry Wadsworth Longfellow	Mark Twain	
	O. Henry	

You will need to use a variety of sources to complete this assignment. The Research Paper must be 4-6 pages in total length, double-spaced (12 pt. Times New Roman font with 1-inch margins), including a cover page and an MLA-style Works Cited page (so at least 4 pages of actual writing).

NAME: _____ GRADE: _____

Due date and schedule tracking guide

Date Due	Assignment Due	Pts.	Points Credited and Teacher Signature
Week 1	Topic Chosen and Controlling Idea [thesis statement] due (typed or neatly written in packet)		
Week 2	Section 1, 2, and 3, 4 from source		
Week 3	Complete sections and begin writing paragraphs per the outline		
Week 4	Work on completing sections and putting paper in for correct paper format with a bibliography		
Week 5-6	Paper due!		
	TEACHER COMMENTS:		FINAL GRADE

(Turn a copy of this sheet in as part of your final paper)

PLAGIARISM: A Warning

Plagiarism is a form of academic dishonesty that robs the intellectual property of others. Plagiarism is NEVER acceptable. <u>A research paper showing evidence of plagiarism will receive a grade of zero with no chance of raising the score, and a discipline referral</u>. This includes AI and ChatGPT. Remember – if you can find papers or passages to copy on the internet, your teacher can find them, too.

What is Plagiarism

Many people think of plagiarism as copying another's work, or borrowing someone else's original ideas. But terms like "copying" and "borrowing" can disguise the seriousness of the offense:

According to the Merriam-Webster Online Dictionary, to "plagiarize" means

1. to steal and pass off (the ideas or words of another) as one's own
2. to use (another's production) without crediting the source
3. to commit literary theft
4. to present as new and original an idea or product derived from an existing source.

In other words, plagiarism is an act of fraud. It involves both stealing someone else's work and lying about it afterward.

But can words and ideas really be stolen?

According to U.S. law, the answer is yes. The expression of original ideas is considered intellectual property, and is protected by copyright laws, just like original inventions. Almost all forms of expression fall under copyright protection as long as they are recorded in some way (such as a book or a computer file).

All of the following are considered plagiarism:

- turning in someone else's work as your own
- copying words or ideas from someone else without giving credit
- failing to put a quotation in quotation marks
- giving incorrect information about the source of a quotation
- changing words but copying the sentence structure of a source without giving credit
- copying so many words or ideas from a source that it makes up the majority of your work, whether you give credit or not.

Most cases of plagiarism can be avoided, however, by citing sources. Simply acknowledging that certain material has been borrowed, and providing your audience with the information necessary to find that source, is usually enough to prevent plagiarism.

Source of the above information: www.plagiarism.org

MLA Citation Format

BOOKS

Format: Author: <u>Title: Subtitle</u>. Place: Publisher, Date.

Examples:

Smith, John. <u>Patience: My Story</u>. New York: Random House, 2001.

Smith, Monica A., and John Jordan. <u>How to Use What You've Got To Get What You Want</u>. Washington, DC: Grolier Publishing, 2000.

MAGAZINE & NEWSPAPER ARTICLES

Format: Author, "Title of Article." <u>Title of Periodical</u> Date: First page-last page.

Examples:

Seinfeld, Jerry. "What I Did Today." <u>People</u> 4 Dec. 1997: A10.

Jackson, Michael and Lisa Marie Presley. "Why We Got Married." <u>National Enquirer</u> 01 Feb. 1998: 4-5.

ARTICLE FROM A REFERENCE BOOK

Format: Author. "Title of Article." <u>Book title: Subtitle</u>. Editor. Place: Publisher, Date. First page-last page. [Simply omit any information that isn't available]

Examples:

King, Martin Luther, "I Have A Dream" <u>Speeches: The Collected Wisdom of Martin Luther King</u>. James Horn. Washington: King Press, 1971. 10-11.

WEBSITE OR WEBPAGE

Format: Author. <u>Title</u>. Editor. Date. Institution. Access Date <URL>. [Omit any information that isn't available]

Examples:

<u>Student Initiated Drinking and Driving Prevention</u>. 4 Oct. 2000. National GRADD. 16 Feb. 2001 <http://www.saferide.org>.

Various contributors. <u>How To Be Popular In High School</u>. Jeff Marx Books. 16 Feb. 2001 <http://www.schoolelection.com/www.popularity.com/>.

MAGAZINE & NEWSPAPER ARTICLES ACCESSED ONLINE

Format:

Author, "Article Title." <u>Periodical</u> Date of article. Access Date <URL>.

[Simply omit any information that isn't available]

Examples:

"Customer's Attempt To Complain To Manager Thwarted By Employee." <u>The Onion</u> 14 Feb. 2001 <http://theonion.com/onion3705/attempt_to_complain.html>.

Carlson, Margaret. "When a Buddy Movie Goes Bad: Bill and Al, the Boys on the Bus-how long ago that seems." <u>Time</u> 19 Feb. 2001. 21 Feb. 2001 http://www.time.com/time/magazine/article/0,9171,98988,00.html

Using Quotes Correctly

In The Crucible John Proctor said, "I say – I say – God is dead!" (111).

During the holocaust the Germans "committed unthinkable acts against humanity" (Price 26).

"In search of a better life, Nelson Mandela strived for equal rights," remarks Professor Jenkins (26).

SAVE YOURSELF EXTRA WORK by…

…using www.citationmachine.net to format your in-text citations and Works Cited page. Click MLA in the upper left corner, select your source type (book, encyclodpedia, web page, etc.), enter required information and click submit, and then cut and past the formatted information into your research paper.

Website Evaluation Criteria Checklist

I. Authority

Is there an author?
Is the author qualified? An expert?
Who is the sponsor? Is it someone reputable?
Is there a link to information about the author or the sponsor?
If the page includes neither a signature nor indicates a sponsor, is there any other way to determine its origin?

II. Accuracy

Is the information reliable and error-free?
Is there an editor or someone who verifies/checks the information?
Do any other sources have the same information?

III. Objectivity

Does the information show a minimum of bias?
Is the page designed to influence your opinion?
Are there any ads on the page?

IV. Currency

Is the page dated?
If so, when was the last update?
How current are the links? Have some expired or moved?

V. Coverage

What topics are covered?
What does this page offer that is not found elsewhere?
How in-depth is the material?

Developing a Thesis Statement(Controlling Idea)

The following examples show how to develop a thesis statement from a broad, general idea. Each step shows a further narrowing of the topic in order to arrive at a legitimate thesis statement.

THESIS: Huck's departure at the end of the novel reflects Twain's own dissatisfaction

with civilization.

THESIS: An extended school year would have a positive effect on learning, student attitudes toward school, and the retention of skills from year to year.

WHAT A THESIS STATEMENT SHOULD NOT BE:

1. A topic or subject by itself cannot serve as a thesis statement. That information tells what the paper is about, but not what you and your research have to say about it.

2. A question cannot serve as a thesis statement because it is not a statement. A question merely says that an answer will follow. However, a question-and-answer pair can be a thesis statement.

3. A general statement that lacks a detailed point of view cannot serve as a thesis statement. A general statement may give the reader background information but does not reflect your point of view.

4. A "so what?" statement. This kind of thesis statement is too obvious (common knowledge) and demonstrates no originality of thought.

WHAT A THESIS STATEMENT SHOULD BE:

1. A complete sentence or two summarizing the point of view in your paper.

2. A specific declaration of your main idea.

3. A statement reflecting your position.

EXAMPLES:

THESIS: *The Midwife's Apprentice* is a realistic interpretation of the Middle Ages, showing what life was really like for the common villager.

THESIS: Throughout *To Kill A Mockingbird* we see Scout Finch mature as she becomes aware of the true nature of the people in her town.

HINT: You write a thesis statement early to focus your attention – not that of your reader. Therefore, as you do your research, you may wish to modify your statement or radically change it (and perhaps you should). That's okay, but you need to discuss a major change with your teacher.

Your Thesis Statement

*First, Jot down your author:_____

*Second, What type of influence did this author have?_____

*Third, Choose a theme that the author addresses in his/her work (you may use previous writing/activities from the class to help you with this): _____

_____

*Choose a second theme that the author addresses in his/her work (you may use previous writing/activities from the class to help you with this): _____

_____

* In what Literary Period did this author write? _____

Now, Fill in the blanks:

_____ and his/her development as a writer affected American

Literature by focusing on the themes of _____ and _____,

reflecting the _____ literary period.

Write this out as one full sentence here:

_____

_____

The Full outline for your paper follows, and consider each box 1-2 paragraphs

Literature Review Notes for crafting your essay paragraphs:

<u>#1: Early Biographical Information: Birthdate, early life and education - locate 1 source</u>

1.

2.

3.

4.

5.

6.

Source:

<u>#2: Influences in writing career: who did your author read? Admire? Correspond with? What is the</u>
<u>writer's literary period and genre? – use a 2nd source</u>

1.

2.

3.

4.

5.

Your sentence on how this information shaped your author's writing:

Source:

#3: Significant Characters and their purpose- include page numbers and a quoted phrase about the character. Identify if the characters represents a theme or the literary period.

1. Character

Quote:

Sentence about the character's significance:

2. Character

Quote:

Sentence about the character's significance

3. Character

Quote:

Sentence about the character's significance

#4: Significant Settings and a statement about their significance (include page numbers)

1. Setting/Location:

Quote:

Sentence about significance

2. Setting/Location:

Quote:

Sentence about significance

3. Setting/Location:

Quote:

Sentence about significance

#5: Brief Statement of Key plot elements that contribute to theme or literary period – include specific quotes from the text with page numbers.

1. Type of plot device/conflict/ device

Quote:

Significance:

2. Type of plot device/conflict/ device

Quote:

Significance:

3. Type of plot device/conflict/ device

Quote:

Significance:

#6: Brief statements about the themes you are addressing in the text

1. First theme:

Quote that shows the theme:

Devices, elements, characters that show the theme

Sentence about significance:

2. First theme:

Quote that shows the theme:

Devices, elements, characters that show the theme

Sentence about significance:

#7: Identify symbols that are important to the themes and literary period (include page numbers and identify which)

1. Common associations with that symbol:

What does the symbol mean for the text:

How does it contribute to the theme

2. Common associations with that symbol:

What does the symbol mean for the text:

How does it contribute to the theme

3. Common associations with that symbol:

What does the symbol mean for the text:

How does it contribute to the theme

#8: Use Researched Sources for this section – include source title, author, and page number in these notes --- Quotations of interest about the text, themes, or literary period (identify which) Then put the quote in the appropriate section 1-7 above

1. Author: _____ Title: _____

Pg # _____ Theme/Literary Period: _____

Quote:

Your statement about this quote:

2. Author: _____ **Title:** _____

Pg # _____ **Theme/Literary Period:** _____

Quote:

Your statement about this quote:

3. Author: _____ **Title:** _____

Pg # _____ **Theme/Literary Period:** _____

Quote:

Your statement about this quote:

How to develop and organize your paragraphs -- English Research Paper Outline:

For sections 3-8, put theme #1 information together, theme #2 information together, and Literary Period information together for parts 4-6 below. Use the second text information to write a paragraph or two on similarities and differences between the two texts. Use the outline below and the notes in the sections above to begin writing rough draft paragraphs for your paper.

1. **Introduction and Controlling Idea (Thesis Statement) –paragraph 1**
    Write down any points you want to include in your introduction in this space. *("Controlling Idea" is just another term for thesis statement or main idea of your research paper. In your final draft, this will come at end of introduction).*

2. **Paragraphs 2-3 - Use sections 1 and 2 for these paragraphs**
    (Biographical information with sources. Have one paragraph on early background information, and the second paragraph on the early writing career and influences and their literary period).

3. **Paragraph #4-5 Significant setting, characters and their motives**
    (Use sections 3-4 information here)

4. **Paragraphs #6-7   Key plot and literary developments in the text.**
    (Use sections 5 information here)

5. **Paragraphs #8-9 - Theme and images from the text**
    (Use sections 6-7 information here)

6. **Conclusion paragraph 10**
    (Use this space to write down any points you want to include in your conclusion. You may write the actual concluding paragraph or simply make bullet-point comments).

7. **List of sources – separate page.**
    (List the sources you have consulted so far. You do not have to use MLA style here – just list book titles, websites, etc).

Research Paper Final Draft Expectations

1. Research Paper is typed, double-spaced, 12 point font, and a normal font type (Times New Roman is the best – this is the default font in Microsoft Word). Margins should be standard 1-inch margins. The Research Paper should look professional – not wrinkled, misprinted, or damaged

2. You should have a cover page with your NAME, DATE, CLASS, and RESEARCH TOPIC. Feel free to add designs or art to the cover.

3. Your research paper must be at least 6 typed pages in total, including the "Works Cited" page and the cover page (*at least 6-9 pages of actual writing*). It should not exceed 9 pages.

4. You must use quotations and proper MLA citation form. You should have **at least 14 citations** total. Ex. According to Smith, the Middle Ages were "a very exciting time" (46). **You must use at least 10 direct quotes from sources – including your text.**

5. You must include a **Works Cited page** at the end of your paper. This is where you list the sources you have cited in your writing. They are listed alphabetically as in a bibliography page. **You will have at least 6 sources listed.** At least **one source must be the book/ text by the author you are writing about.**

6. First Drafts/outlines – let your teacher review it and provide feedback.

7. Research Papers turned in late will lose 5 points every day.

8. Check your printer well before it is expected to perform. Printers that are out of ink or don't work correctly will not constitute a legitimate excuse. Also, computers that fail will not be excused. Save your work often - on both your hard drive and a CD/floppy drive/flash drive. Better yet, save it to the school H-drive, so you can print it here.

NAME: _____   GRADE: _____

Research Paper FINAL DRAFT Grading Rubric (200 points total)

Turn a copy page in with your final draft for grading!

1. Paper is neatly presented & follows   Yes   No   / 25 pts.

    Format (turn in page 2):

2. There are at least 10 citations   Yes   No   / 25 pts.

    (with 2-3 direct quotes) & five sources on "Works Cited" page

    and one web source evaluated):

3. A clear thesis is stated (turn in page 7): Yes   No   / 25 pts.

4. Literary analysis is developed and defended well   5 4 3 2 1   / 40 pts.

    & writing is original:

5. All points from the packet outline are

    Addressed thoroughly (turn in pages 8-10)   5 4 3 2 1   / 40pts

6. Language and writing is dynamic: 5 4 3 2 1   / 25pts

7. Mechanics (spelling & grammar) are   5 4 3 2 1   / 20 pts.

    error free:

                                          Total: / 200 POINTS

Made in the USA
Columbia, SC
04 September 2024